HORACE'S HOPE

Theodore R. Sizer

HORACE'S HOPE
What Works for the American High School

Houghton Mifflin Company
Boston   New York   1996

For information about permission to reproduce selections from this book,
write to Permissions, Houghton Mifflin Company, 215 Park Avenue South,
New York, New York 10003.

For information about this and other Houghton Mifflin trade and reference books and
multimedia products, visit The Bookstore at Houghton Mifflin on the World Wide Web
at http://www.hmco.com/trade/.

Library of Congress Cataloging-in-Publication Data
Sizer, Theodore R.
    Horace's hope : what works for the American high school / Theodore R. Sizer
        p.   cm.
    Includes bibliographical references (p.)
ISBN 0-395-73983-7
1. High Schools — United States. 2. Education, Secondary — United States —
Aims and objectives. 3. Educational change — United States.   I. Title.
    LA222.S543 1996
    373.73 — dc20   95-47702   CIP

Printed in the United States of America

QUM 10 9 8 7 6 5 4 3 2 1

For my wife, Nancy; for our children,
Tod and Rebecca, Judy, Hal and Susan, and Lyde and Jim;
for our grandchildren, Cally, Lyde, Teddy, Julie, and Nicholas;
and especially for Jay and David, members of our family
who have arrived since Horace Smith set about
redesigning Franklin High School

Contents

Contents

Preface

Horace Smith

HORACE SMITH is a veteran high school English teacher, respected by his colleagues, revered by some of his students, and compulsive in his love of his trade and the place at which he plies it, Franklin High School.

Horace is not a real person but my invention, an amalgam of teachers whom I met during visits to secondary schools across the country during the early 1980s. For my purposes, he represents the best of the teaching force. Horace is male and female, black and white and Asian and Latino, a science teacher, a coach, a counselor, a mathematics teacher. If there could be an Every High School U.S.A., Franklin High School would be that.

In watching and listening to Horace Smith (in his myriad manifestations) fifteen years ago, I saw with ever-increasing clarity the compromises forced on him by his school's familiar regimen, compromises that profoundly and negatively affected his work. Horace knew that the routines of the school forced him to teach in ways that he knew were second class. That is, he had to compromise his standards.

Each year he had 120 different youngsters to get to know. He saw each one fleetingly almost every day, but almost always as part of a class with twenty to thirty other kids. Each class was but a sliver of time, forty-plus minutes preceded and followed by bells and bedlam in the hallways. Horace knew some of his students well but most of them only as semi-strangers passing through. He put up a good front, though. *I know my kids,* he would tell everyone, especially their parents. He knew that this was a lie but could not bring himself to admit it.

The school processed those young people, marching them through a school day that rarely changed its shape or pace, organizing them by their ages and the scores they made on tests, rewarding them on the basis of grades that represented no common standard among Franklin High School's faculty, and passing them on to college or work on the basis of credentials that were part fibs, part truths, and a nest of numbers which had little correlation with the talents and commitments that were actually necessary in the lives to which they were all headed.

Orderliness in the school was a fetish. Quiet was golden. A "good" class had children leaning over their desks, appearing to work diligently. The fact that most were quietly bored or seething with resentment or simply turned off made no difference. Most of Franklin's kids merely went through the expected motions. Getting the diploma was a goal for many of them, and they knew that if they appeared to be dutiful, showed up, and did something in class, they would collect their credits and graduate. Like their predecessors, Horace and his colleagues simply let them get away with that. To fight for something better would call for an enormous battle. The public and the profession preferred to let the sleeping dog of mindless schoolwork lie.

Franklin High School tried hard to be everything to everyone. The list of school goals was as long as it was pretentious, running from the academic to the personal, from mastery of science to the development of self-confidence and a principled life. The school day was a jumble of activities, and the most prominent students were involved in a blizzard of programs — AP physics, cheerleading, the yearbook, the homecoming committee, choir, senior social studies, and more, all at once. The more you did, the better. The quality of the academic and extracurricular work was an afterthought, save in a few places such as varsity athletics. For a student, being busy in all sorts of activity was a virtue, being known for this breathless visibility was a jewel.

Horace understood all this busy overload of obligations. He spoke of it rarely, however. The basic incongruity, even mindlessness, of the Franklin regimen represented too much to confront at once.

Franklin's daily schedule was a marvel of complexity. Every teacher had to lope from this to that to keep up. Twenty minutes for lunch, if you were lucky. No time to talk with colleagues at length about anything of importance. Barely enough time after school to read and grade all those students' papers, not to mention work at the second job that many teachers had to take on to meet their families' budgets.

How then could anyone change such a diabolically complicated system? Tackling one piece would affect every other piece. The political wars within the school and among each program's special-interest groups would be ferocious. Sorting out this complexity and setting sensible priorities would take faculty time, of which there was little.

The traditional system seemingly conspired against change, and it was not only the school boards' and administrators' fault. The union leaders, Horace's close friends, tacitly accepted the mindlessness as much as any other group. The colleges' education professors went along too, preparing recruits in the old ways for jobs that Horace knew they could never do well. Horace found few kindred spirits with whom to ally in any sort of bold effort. The widely heralded reform initiatives from the policy community rarely addressed the debilitating compromises. These initiatives appeared to Horace to be voices from afar, singing worthy songs that spoke barely at all to high schools as they in fact were.

At root, apparently, was the implicit belief that significant reform was impossible. High school was high school. There could be tinkering here, a modestly new course of study there, an after-school program added, new tests applied, new curriculum frameworks distributed, fiery speeches given by outraged political leaders, fingers pointed. However, the compromises of the past would remain the compromises of the future. Whatever new directives came from above, they would have to be addressed within the existing system, and the existing system was overloaded, dysfunctional, and shaped to make almost any change exceedingly difficult to accomplish.

Yet, perhaps paradoxically, Horace Smith kept going. He found ways to provide some of his students with a serious education, in Horace's case within Franklin High School's theater program. It was his delight in the accomplishment and friendship of these adolescents that brought him sustaining energy. "Let me tell you about . . . ," he would say to me, and the story of a particular youngster would tumble out. However, only a fraction of the children could become such a particular person for Horace. There was not time, nor did the school give any incentive for such attention. He resented that so much that he barely acknowledged it.

Horace Smith provides the lens through which I have viewed American secondary education over the past decade and a half. Such a perch was and is natural for me. In 1981 I had just completed nine years as a high school principal and history teacher, and I was intensely aware of the nature and craft of school-keeping, the incessant, fascinating dailiness of that craft, and the wonderful specialness of adolescents. The lens fit.

The angle from which one views schools matters. Horace's compromises, and the need to address them, have provided for me not only the scaffolding of an argument but a set of priorities, ones that inform what is now a large reform effort, the Coalition of Essential Schools. Horace's angle of vision has encouraged me to pursue change in ways somewhat different from traditional reform activity. I respect the wonderful (and inevitable) idiosyncrasy of each school. Accordingly, I take a less precise tack than what is generally expected — less prescriptive, driven more by persuasion than by pressure, primarily dependent on the initiative of the Horace Smiths and the culture of the localities where the particular schools are.

Of course, the view from the classroom is not the only view to take; but it is a crucial view. Horace's compromises have been seriously ignored in action, if not in discussion, about American educational policy. Failure to understand what bedevils Horace Smith and then to do something about it guarantees the failure of reform. Such a view colors the very name of our Coalition's effort — *essential* schools.

I have written in *Horace's Compromise* of the high schools as I saw them during my 1980s travels. In 1992 I published a portrait *(Horace's School)* of what one specific approach to addressing those compromises might take, an example of an Essential school. *Horace's Hope* is my meditation on what we may have learned over the last years of serious effort at high school reform.

Seeing reform primarily through Horace's eyes has provoked several themes, ones that this book deals with in some detail.

The heart of schooling is found in relationships between student, teacher, and ideas. Kids differ, and serious ideas affect each one in often interestingly different ways, especially as that child matures.

Horace painfully knows that one cannot teach a student well if one does not know that student well. If the task is the mere memorization of simple lists, maybe, or the development of a routine skill. Serious understanding of an important and complex issue, the stuff of good secondary education? Rarely, if ever.

Parents as well as teachers know this. Private schools and schools in affluent suburbs know this ("We offer small classes"). Every parent I have dealt with in forty years of teaching, without exception, has expected me to know her or his child well. This is a sensible and reasonable expectation.

The traditional assembly-line metaphor for schooling does not work. Kids are not on conveyer belts, with teachers hanging knowledge on them as they pass by. Schools do not "deliver instructional services," pumping up intellectual tires and delivering pedagogical pizza. Children — blessedly — are more complicated and thus more interesting than that.

The existing apparatus of testing ("assessment" is the word in vogue) is seriously flawed, giving us at best snippets of knowledge about a student and at worst a profoundly distorted view of that child. Americans have long put too much dependence on the fledgling science of testing — the plumbing of a human mind and the prediction of the future capability of that mind — and never more so than at present.

There is virtually no evidence, save at the extremes, that most of the scores of which we make so much correlate very much at all with a young person's future activity in life. Alas, in spite of this, the political and administrative need for simple measures swamps common sense about what can be measured and how.

Horace is left with the difficult business of carefully observing and assessing each student's actual work. He deals in the academic realm in the same one-by-one way — looking at each student's real performance — that athletic coaches and music teachers do. No coach ever fielded a team and no music teacher ever assembled an orchestra on the basis of a set of scores. It is the student's actual and sustained performance on the field or behind the tuba that counts, not just what that student did with a pencil and paper at one sitting. Horace deeply resents the categorization of his students' minds on such a basis.

I have learned that being vocally skeptical of tests labels me as being "against standards." Such a charge is bizarre. Low-standard assessment in the quest for high standards is a terrible irony, and inflicting it on children is an outrage.

America's fetish about tests masks profound differences of opinion about the academic ends of education, especially in the senior high school. Horace copes with this daily. Is it enough merely to know that Richard Nixon was president from 1969 to 1974, when he resigned? Or are the facts that led to his resignation important too? And what about the facts made available in the books at school: does Franklin High School's library have all of the data necessary to explain fully what happened, and if not, what facts are yet to be gathered? Indeed, what might a "fact" in this situation be? What does the matter of Nixon's resignation tell us about the American presidency, about the culture of the early 1970s, about our political system? How, then, does one approach Oliver Stone's movie *Nixon*? Does carefully studying Nixon's final months in the White House imbue a young person with the habit of looking at such a major political happening — with skepticism, reserve, an understanding about such matters?

Horace believes that all such levels of understanding and habit are important, necessary objectives for a senior high school. Many disagree with him, asserting that the "facts" alone are what school should be about. A student's opinion and how he assembles and supports it, they say, are beyond the scope of school. School is about What Is. Others may say that because we cannot measure habits, they should have no bearing on an assessment of a student's merit. Still others will argue that a student's habits are not the school's business.

The recent national debates over educational standards have served to reveal some of these differences. They are profound ones. Horace lives with them daily. He resents those who imply that America clearly agrees on what the substance and standard of serious schooling in fact might be.

Horace also knows that adolescents gain much of their education outside school. They will spend more hours with Richard Nixon at *Nixon* than they will in class. They hear more and experience more in the street, on a job, at home, from the television, from the computer than in school. Going to school for many kids is an expected routine, little more. Horace engages his classes in conversations that are profoundly influenced by the talk of the street and over the air and via the telephone lines. Oprah and O.J., the video arcade and the Internet count, big time. Against them, Horace has a struggle.

Franklin High School is part of a school system. Horace knows that system's strength. It decides what he will be paid and when he will work, gives him what it thinks he needs, and shelters him from the public. At its best, it struggles to lessen his compromises. Usually it is simply fickle. Its leaders, often estimable men and women, come and go with alarming speed. Able though most are, the boat that they are asked to steer is built to swamp them any time they stray too far from accepted courses.

The stability in public education comes from the extraordinary inertia of traditional practice. Pressure for change, whether wise or unwise, ultimately emerges as hiccups — a new curriculum is recommended here, a new test there, some interesting professional development somewhere else — but by and large leaves the schools' design and routines much as they are now. Bolder change would shake up one or another pressure group and would thus require sustained leadership. Those whom the system usually accepts as its stakeholders seem to be arranged to check one another continually, to cancel any initiative. When Horace bothers to think at all about this issue (which is rarely), he wonders why some of those who claim to be stakeholders — people who are not directly affected by decisions in schools — deserve the attention and power the system affords them. Those who have to live with the compromises should, he muses, have a greater incentive to change them.

There is no standard Franklin High. The people who are Horace teach in many settings, and the differences among them, usually defined by the economic class of the students, are striking. "Equal educational opportunity" is a cruel joke, Horace knows. Districts with schools with puny libraries abut districts that have schools with vast libraries. Some schools are palaces, some are leaky relics of decades of neglect. The savage inequality of which Jonathan Kozol so powerfully wrote is so deeply established in American school practice that it plays remarkably little role in public discussion.[1] Horace pays little attention to it; it is just the way we do things in this country, he implies. Inequality is the one best expression of local control.

Someone like me who has the luxury of traveling among schools sees this inequity powerfully. If America has any civic standards, two of the most important are fairness and generosity. Both of these are mocked by the practice of American education. No other industrial nation in the world tolerates such inequities. No other industrial nation will pay so heavily for their long-range costs. That reality alone should be an embarrassment for Americans. However, we largely shrug it off. There seems little rage here, not even in Horace, who is fully occupied with trying to confront the needs in his own back yard.

And yet Horace has hope. He is stubborn. His students are remarkably resilient. He knows why he gets up in the morning: the careers of many of his students are sweet dividends to his life. He enjoys many of his colleagues, especially those who like to learn, to think, to use language, to figure out kids. Even the mordant among them have kept a sense of humor and a willingness to work hard. The carping cynics, so familiar, can be tolerated.

In recent years, there has been some movement. Some of the plans for Franklin High School did take root, ones that addressed the most nagging compromises. People like Horace in other Franklin High Schools appeared to be ready to move beyond their restlessness, and they found unexpected support among some parents of their students. Their collective activity — the result of the boiling-over of impatience with the compromises — had promise. The larger system, strangled in its own problems, lacked the will either to stifle or vigorously to promote serious new ideas. There was in effect a vacuum. The hope resided there, in the belief that such a vacuum could be constructively filled.

Horace knew that all this would take time, particularly because the changes contemplated were not merely ones of structure and practice. They affected the very way teachers and students and parents viewed serious secondary education. The reform was above all a reform of ideas. That would take a generation to root, and the rooting would be uneven and messy. However, it would be fundamental, and fundamental change is what Horace knew was required.

From such a schoolteacher's vantage point was this book written. It is only one vantage point. However, none is more important.

Note: A fuller account of A Study of High Schools, from which *Horace's Compromise* emerged, and the Coalition of Essential Schools appears in the appendix.

As in my two previous Horace books, I have used the device of nonfiction fiction. Save for the portraits of a few Essential schools — ones chosen from among dozens of equally revealing examples — that fall between chapters, all the descriptions of real schools, teachers, and students are masked and sometimes interwoven. The resulting word pictures are thus imaginary, but in their details they are wholly real. This writer's device allows me to render descriptions that are to my most careful eye authentic without making sharp and thus sometimes unflattering identifications.

HORACE'S HOPE

1

A Story Where Nothing Happens

GIVEN ALL the controversy over the past two decades about the effectiveness of American high schools, I have wondered just what has changed as a result of all the public and political concern. My hunch — widely shared, sad to say — was that not much had altered. To test this hunch informally, during the fall of 1994 I revisited several schools I had gone to in 1981 as part of my research for A Study of High Schools. I wanted to sense what was different and what was the same there, and to learn whether all the talk about reform had made a difference and if so, what was visibly different.

I chose a few schools with which I had had no intervening contact, places that were not members of the Coalition of Essential Schools or an analogous effort. That is, these were typical schools, pressing forward in ordinary ways, subject to their districts' and states' authority without any particular, focused outside force, resources, or advocacy.

One in particular stood out as representative: Tillson High School, which in 1981 was the largest secondary school in a major industrial city. Thirty-eight hundred young people then filled its sprawling building, a vast and impressive structure barely able to contain even those students actually in attendance. Crowds of adolescents dominated the hallways, noisy, jovial, pushing and joshing.

The cabdriver who took me from my hotel out to the school that autumn morning thirteen years ago was incredulous at my supposed courage. My field notes from the visit record his warnings: "Better let me pick you up when you are through out there — no cabs in that part of town. That is a bad neighborhood. People like you should not be out there."

Vivid memories of the visit still remain in my mind — memories of the paradoxes of a grand high school that serves the children of the poor. At Tillson I found decent adults serving needy but wonderfully energetic kids, without excuse and with a commitment that was almost religious in its zeal. At the same time, these same people were suffused with cynicism and complaint.

The rushed, carefully orchestrated, and at times utterly bizarre daily schedule was accepted as though it were as inevitable and normal as the rising of the sun. Tillson was for many kids an island of order and sensitivity in otherwise turbulent lives, but it was driven by routines that, however comfortable in their predictability, made little sense.

Tillson's adults were extraordinarily mindful of some of the kids, although they worked in an institution of extraordinary mindlessness. Most memorable was the principal, a giant of a man, Gil Carter. My field notes record images of him.[1]

> The principal is an Old Testament prophet, a powerful charismatic and articulate man. Like "99.999 percent" of his school (his words) he is black, and he has been principal of Tillson for almost a decade. He is in constant motion and handles many things directly — which is one reason why he has to reach frequently for his blue Maalox bottle to handle his ulcer. . . . Gil shares his small office with his most senior assistant principal, "Hobie" (Hubert) Ewell. Their desks are side by side, and three phones seem to be constantly ringing, one on Gil's desk, one on Hobie's, and one — covered with red tape — behind Gil's desk. The red phone is the panic phone and is the private line direct to the central office and regional people.
>
> In the total of an hour which I spent in that office over the course of the day, I saw students, most of them there for a chat rather than business; teachers with problems having to do with meetings they

were supposed to attend or with unruly youngsters or with pressure they were under to accept other jobs or with possible attendance at management seminars; the regional superintendent, who burst in without knocking with some crisis on his mind, and who was the one person who successfully dragged Gil from behind his desk so that the conversation was not eavesdropped on by the four or five other people who happened to be in the office at the same time. . . .

Gil is clearly "the man" in this school, and he dispenses wisdom, love, and patronage in great gobs in a memorable way. A conversation in that office was a marvel to conduct. One person would roll a question out along the floor, Gil would answer it until a phone rang or until somebody else walked in, at which point Hobie would pick up Gil's comments mid-sentence, as though nothing had happened.

What I saw was genial and effective, if visibly chaotic, crisis management, with most of the "crises" having to do with the immediate problems of adults. Gil kept the lid on, kept the place going — not changing, not rethinking, not reforming, but *going,* getting from 7:45 A.M. to 3:30 P.M. without too much hassle, and he did it, thanks to his enthusiastic magnetism, with wisdom and gusto.

During that 1981 visit, the teachers told me, sadly, that they sensed a decline, that the improvements and optimism they had experienced in the late 1970s (probably owing to the last surge of War on Poverty programs passing through the system) were abating. A white home economics teacher tried to explain: it was "because we have kids who are sort of raunchy." She could not tell me precisely what she meant by "raunchy" (an old-fashioned word to hear in schools, however apt it might have been), save that "the place is getting pulled apart" by kids coming from seriously dysfunctional homes. "We have fights, but we don't have what you have been reading about. Other schools in the city have that. Kids in high school ought to be heard — they are entitled to be heard," the teacher said. "When kids come in for discipline, it's usually for something else. I don't mollycoddle kids. I don't buy the racism argument. That's why I get along with black parents."

Other teachers at Tillson told me of the poor reading abilities of many kids and their indifference to school: "Kids don't see the purpose of working hard. They get promoted anyway." Attendance in classes was low, especially during first and eighth period; a typical class when I visited had seventeen kids at their desks and thirty-five on the teacher's roster. This did not square with Tillson's reported attendance statistics, which were much higher. (From that and many similar experiences in other schools over the past years, I have developed a virtually total distrust of any numbers coming out of school bureaucracies; the majority are likely to be sheer fiction.)

I listened to a group of teachers and recorded in my notes that "we talked of teacher load. If every student came every day, a teacher would see 175 kids. The contract calls for no fewer and no more than 35 kids per class. While 'many kids don't show,' the teachers told me, 'you are responsible for them all.' The numbers are staggering. It's a credit to the students that there hasn't been an explosion."

I visited six of Tillson's biology classes, back to back. None had more than seventeen students; some had fewer than ten. The laboratories were well equipped for such small numbers, but the teaching was "on the whole deadly," I wrote. There was the "usual list of words written on the blackboard, with the kids writing them down in notebooks or on scraps of paper. It was fact-stuffing supreme, that apparent plague of all beginning biology instruction. No wonder so few youngsters survive that tenth-grade biology course to go on in science! The work was dry, totally empty of any sort of life." I talked of this, gingerly, with the teachers. "We are partly to blame," they agreed, and they repeated the often-heard theme that the kids didn't care, that they saw no purpose in schooling.

Although both the teachers and Gil mentioned the standardized, state-required minimum competency tests that had just been mandated, they made little of this prospect. Standardized examinations of one sort or another had long been in place, and were taken by whoever showed up on the examining day.

I visited two special programs, one just launched to serve the "academically talented" and the other the Junior Reserve Officer Training Corps (JROTC) unit. The Accelerated Program was the brainchild of a guidance counselor and enrolled some 160 tenth-graders who had been identified as academically able and religious in their attendance. The kids were to take a focused core program, including Latin. The first cohort, now in the eleventh grade, numbered 155. Such a program, I was told, "is good for the neighborhood. The good neighborhood kids can come to their school now." Tillson runs this alternative, Gil told me, whereas other school-within-a-school programs in the city are administered at long range by the district's central office.

Students in the JROTC had recently been given some limited security duties because the professional safety officers had been fired under Reagan administration cutbacks. Led by a solid retired army sergeant, the corps had a nice élan, a place to meet (and the cadets seemed to be there often, chatting with the staff), and an in-school (under the eaves) air-rifle range for target practice. Half of the cadets were girls.

Federal programs came in for a good deal of criticism from the teachers. The head of one department was all for the Reagan administration's cuts: they might, she hoped, get rid of what she called boondoggles. She told me of the layers of committees appointed to oversee the teachers' and students' work and how each committee avoided paying any attention to any other committee. What did she do at the school level? "I lie like hell — it fits my philosophy," by which she meant that she went ahead and did what she wanted. "If you have good people," she argued, "give them some respect, some professional attitude."

My field notes ended with a summary paragraph. I described Tillson as

> a large, complex institution with the principal at the center, a man holding control over the school by the force of his very considerable personality. The control does not extend, obviously, to the dozens and dozens who skip school; the problem of no-shows is far more severe than even the honest Gil Carter will admit. Those 50 percent absentee rates in biology class are a measure of the difficulty the school faces. For the kids who show up, the game is played: classes are held, notes dictated, tests given, the routine is pushed along. One gets no sense that the kids are challenged or that there is the kind of yeasty angularity which makes for a good school. Tillson is not a frightening or frightful place; many of the

adults — probably most of them — care for the kids, and the kids realize this. But that is not enough — as Carter knows — and the improvement will require a lot more than good will and a prophet prowling the halls making kids feel good about themselves.

A Tillson teacher used a word to describe his own and his colleagues' work that still haunts me. It was all "a conspiracy," he said, a tacit arrangement among all who showed up at the building to get along; no one would push another very much, no one would tell the truth when it could remain unspoken, no one would dare to ask about implications for tomorrow. Tillson was a vast, well-intentioned, conspiratorial theater, a place for the kids to spend time as they passed through adolescence into "life," whatever that might have in store for each of them.

Much that my colleagues and I observed during the early 1980s for A Study of High Schools was reflected at Tillson. The schedule was the essential engine, which meant that simply getting through the complicated day, with all its bells and hall passings and comings and goings — and thus merely covering the stuff in class, rather than demonstrably learning it — was paramount. School had to keep happening. Appearances and meeting the expected requirements were all. Control was critical in a school like Tillson, which was, after all, the size of a small town.

Tillson worked by its own lights because, as I put it in 1981, Carter kept the school going with his skill at crisis management. This need to control was at the heart of the "conspiracy" that was tacitly worked out by all involved. "I will ask the minimum of you if you will quietly support me with the authorities," the deal went. What resulted was the kind of compromise that so sapped the morale of Horace Smith.

Those staff members who resented the routines worked in effect as loyal saboteurs, not rocking the boat and not going completely off on their own at the same time. "I lie a lot," one honest teacher said. Since visiting Tillson, I have seen that such insubordination is rife in most schools, or at least in those that appear to value the routines over the apparent needs of a particular moment. Some of this insubordination helps children; some does not. The very act — reflecting powerful mistrust, whether justified or not — undermines the kind of community that schools must develop, as I now well know.

I sensed dismay among the faculty at Tillson, their sense of the decline in the students' effort. The special programs that gave some sense of purpose and belonging to some students, such as JROTC, were precarious at best.

Thirteen years later, my recollections of Tillson were contradictory. I had admired the enthusiasm of Gil Carter and some of his people. They were not whiners. They clearly liked their students and relished their jobs. The school sang wherever Gil was. But this singing had been, I remembered, a facade, one unworthy of a man of Gil Carter's commitment. The school ran, but it did not work, in the sense that many students were never or seldom there and that what was placed before them when they were there was hardly engaging.

In 1994, the striking pile of elaborate Herbert Hoover–era stucco and stonework that was Tillson High School seemed much as it had during my earlier visit. The mix of single- and two-family homes surrounding the school, interspersed with fast-food restaurants, gasoline stations, and small businesses, was also as I remembered. The neighborhood's exterior, however, masked the fact that though it had been tough in 1981, it was now far more violent. Gunfire and its consequences were common.

My guide, an associate from the superintendent's office (no taxicab this time), parked among faculty cars close to the entrance to the auto shop classrooms, at the back of the building. By chance we were greeted there by a young teacher, who took us into the building through an inconspicuous, unguarded door. While the long bare hallways and the swirl of litter at their margins were familiar, the human traffic was not. Tillson now had barely 1500 students, down more than 50 percent from the crowd of 1981, as a result of dramatically smaller school enrollments in this declining inner-city neighborhood. As the city's economy ebbed, so did its population, especially the number of families with teenage children.

A wing of the sprawling school had now been taken over for an audiovisual equipment center, but the feel of the place was friendly, not tumultuous. Maybe, I thought, having visited so many big secondary schools around the country, I had become immune to the grand theater of thundering herds of kids in big, strange institutional buildings.

The youngsters passing by, still virtually all African American, were cheerful and noisily adolescent. They appeared not to mind the metal detectors embedded at their entranceway and manned by uniformed security guards. The patrolling JROTC kids whom I had appreciated in 1981 had been relieved of this kind of duty. Today's world was scarier, whatever the budget crisis. Some kids had to be disarmed at the door — not a job for teenagers.

Principal Carter had retired. Samantha Miller, his replacement, met us in a classroom near the front (and for students the only) entrance. Sam, as Samantha was called, was not a visibly authoritative figure, as Gil had been. She too was cheerful, approachable while exuding an "I'm in charge" demeanor. She was fun to be with. She listened to my questions; Gil had often ignored them and answered questions that he wished I had asked.

At the beginning of the schoolday, Sam and an assistant principal were checking in the latecomers one by one, entering the infraction on each student's computer record. The computers rested on trolleys, which were eventually wheeled back into the administrative storeroom. The latecomers — some twenty of them when we arrived — waited quietly at desks in rows. Some slept. The administrators were friendly; there were no sharp reprimands, just a bit of joshing here and there, all with a smile. The kids responded dully; they were subdued, without much affect. Many, we learned, were used to this start-of-the-schoolday routine. One wondered just where each had spent the preceding night, at home or on the street.

Sam Miller stayed with me during the entire morning, roaming the halls, radio in hand (though she never used it in the three hours we spent together). She exchanged a word here with a student and a greeting there with a faculty member. The students all knew her. One youngster asked for an appointment; Sam arranged it on the spot for seven-thirty the next morning. Another showed her a packaged design for her prom dress. As Sam moved on, she rolled her eyes at me over that one. Are there any limits on matters upon which a principal must have an opinion? Her office, into which I later poked my head, seemed smaller than I remembered. No assistant principal shared it with her. It was neat, in repose. The outlying administrative areas had been refurbished and were well lit.

In our march around the building we concentrated on the new things. Windows had been refitted and exterior stonework repointed. The city authorities had instituted an elaborate computer-based citywide student record system, one that allowed an assistant principal or another authorized official to dip into the complete records of each student wherever that student might be enrolled. A standardized record system put the students at the fingertips of anyone with authority in the school system. I wondered what in fact might be the ultimate educational benefit of all this dazzling technology; it struck me as simply a way to keep track of each student, with no obvious action implied to follow that kept track — data for data's sake.

We visited technology labs, some full of students, some virtually empty. We saw the school's new communications studio, where students could "go on TV every day," we were told. We spent a half-hour in a careers office, a brightly lit and centrally located space staffed by an energetic woman who helped students with college and job applications. We visited the library, an impressive space with a soaring high ceiling and with about the same number of books as before, but now with several computer terminals tied into reference networks. There were around a dozen kids in the room at the hour we visited. It was a remarkably still place.

As we wandered through the halls, I wondered what would follow school for these young people. I asked Sam, would there be jobs for them when and if they graduated from high school? The answer was a qualified no. Heavy industry had largely left town, and what remained was highly automated. The kids needed skills, and many lacked them. Tillson was a neighborhood high school; students at the city's magnet secondary schools certainly had a better shot at the few available jobs. Where, then, did the kids go? There was no answer. Later in the day, though, a teacher described to me the best route, at least for the boys, to the middle class: dealing drugs. This was the principal means of getting ahead that these youngsters observed, their one model of security, independence, respect, and a car of their own. It required taking risks and working hard and steadily — nice middle-class virtues — but led, of course, nowhere or to jail or to a cemetery plot. However, it was essentially all that was available.

We dropped in on several new special programs. The Accelerated Program appeared to have given way to an initiative for talented seventh- and eighth-graders, designed in part to get them accustomed to Tillson, in the hope that they might stay there, and in part to use the high school's yawning space. Other programs involved part-time work outside the school.

We visited the large auditorium, still elegant despite its superficial shabbiness and large enough to seat the entire school, so Sam holds periodic schoolwide meetings there. The stage was deep and the acoustics were fine, but money was not available for a theater program. Four kids were playing chess on the stage when we were there, with a teacher in the shadows.

During a break I chatted with four loquacious seniors, young women eager to tell me about their school and, when I asked them, about their futures. Yes, they liked Tillson. They were proud of their school. Yes, they were a bit afraid to graduate. What did they most like about their school? The special programs, both in and out of the building. After graduation? College (nervous giggles). Where? They didn't know. Any ideas about options? Again, they didn't know. Did they have jobs? Yes. Doing what? All were clerks at one store or another. Saving money for college? Oh no, they needed the money now.

This was a happy, friendly group, what one teacher called the "It girls" of the senior class, the ones that many teachers were pushing hard. They liked the attention. They lived in a harsh world. I hoped their cheerful optimism would carry them through.

Back in step with Sam, I visited the JROTC area on the top floor, under the eaves. The shooting range was as I remembered it. A class of ninth-graders was being drilled by an upperclass student officer. Most were girls; the uniformed faculty member in charge, a retired army sergeant first class, said that some 80 percent of the JROTC kids were young women. "The boys don't want the hassle of the discipline," he explained. (I puzzled over this. Did army discipline signal some kind of now-unadmired conformity to the young men?) A clutch of students were shining their brass in anticipation of a detail that afternoon; the school was to be the site for a district-wide workshop about how to drill students in preparation for the metropolitan standardized tests, and the JROTC youngsters were to strut their stuff beforehand.

The importance of testing, something that had been at the fringes of Gil's concerns in 1981, kept creeping into my discussions with Sam and the teachers. There was an urgency I had not sensed in 1981. The upcoming regional accreditation visit, for example, was to focus on "outcomes" and only secondarily on what the school offered. The programs were nice, but did the kids benefit, the accreditors would ask, from those offerings?

Sam Miller appeared to accept the reasonableness of this expectation, but acknowledged that it brought in its wake new and difficult tensions. More poignant was concern from several teachers about the new state testing program, which would largely move away from multiple-choice and fill-in-the-blank questions to essays and problem-oriented exercises. The students had been drilled in how to take the former, the teachers told me, but were utterly unprepared for the latter, and the faculty was receiving no support in trying to ready both themselves and the youngsters for the new kinds of tests. The revolution in test-taking (and the preparation for it) was apparently to be addressed by some process of spontaneous combustion.

I caught a whiff of anger here, and of frustration. Some of the teachers remembered my earlier visit; this was a remarkably stable and veteran faculty, and interested outside visitors to Tillson had been few and far between. What was the same? The loads? Five classes a day, 150 to 175 kids per teacher. The schedule and bells and all that? Just the same. Time for teachers to meet during the day? None to speak of. All was like this in 1981.

Student attendance? Still about 50 percent, at least in their classes, whatever the record-keepers and their computers might report. The curriculum? About the same as I had witnessed in 1981, but some changes were coming down from headquarters. U.S. history, for example, was to be given to a first wave of tenth-graders in one term the following year; the course would cover 1865 to the present. What about Washington and Jefferson and all that? The teachers were not sure. It would come sometime.

Were there materials for this new program? No. Some of the texts were the same ones I saw in 1981. There were only enough for a class at a time. As a result, the students could not take them home; each volume was used over and over again in each successive class. Homework? A shrug. Preparation for what was newly expected? More shrugs.

How were the kids, thirteen years later? It is harder to grow up now, I was told; the world is tougher, the kids more desperate. Teacher morale? Low. The contract is poor, they told me. We are losing salary ground to the suburbs. We are not consulted about reform initiatives. They are presented to us, essentially a fait accompli. And then the central staffers wonder why we are not enthusiastic, they complained.

Sam took me to no classes, and I felt that she wanted it that way. I did not press her. The classroom doors were shut, in any event. Apart from its rejuvenated exterior, its elegant (if limited) technology, and its streamlined administration, Tillson apparently had not changed much in thirteen years. The bells rang as before, and the routines were the familiar ones. The kids were colorful in their enthusiasms as always; the irrepressible and ever hopeful dance of adolescence had not been smothered. But serious learning? The agony of the staff about the testing said it all. They knew that their classes did not prepare students for real academic performance — exhibiting what you know, answering questions about it, puzzling out the answers to questions that test understanding rather than just the retention of facts and symbols. At best, I was told by teachers — usually obliquely (it hurt, obviously) — most current classes prepared the youngsters to take simplistic machine-graded tests and not much more.

The "conspiracy" was still there. The adults and the students came to terms with the deal they had to make to get along. As before, there were some stubbornly caring adults, and there were kids with dreams and the willingness to continue the routines of the school day.

The larger community, those in power in the city, could not really know and appreciate what growing up at Tillson and in its neighborhood was actually like. That they did not know could mean that they did not care, or maybe that they cared more about other things.

The issue of race lay barely below the surface. The economic divide between black and white — and all that that symbolized — was immense here, and growing. The warmth and civility of the African American administrators politely masked the problem, but what were they to do? The unfairness made me shudder. Could we white Americans ever have the courage to acknowledge this blatant distortion of the American creed and do something about it? I kept the query to myself. It was as painfully embarrassing as it was persistent.

Conspiracy, indeed. My central office guide and I drove away from Tillson, wanting to be quiet but inevitably talking as newly met friends do. The recent gubernatorial election, the second coming of the Republicans, the union, the city budget, how the local universities help out, what the new state assessment system would be like — all these were the burning issues of the immediate only, the stuff that dominates educational routines. None dealt with the heart of the problem: how to attract and hold a diverse group of usually very needy kids to the task of preparing themselves to survive well in a harsh and largely uncaring community.

We avoided the deeper questions. Why is a conspiracy deemed so necessary? Why do we, living in the richest nation in the history of the world, tolerate such searing inequality, such corrosive racism? Why do so many Americans shy away from serious school reform? Why is all the reformist rhetoric followed with nothing but trivial action? Why isn't race openly on the policy agenda? Why is the condemnation of public education so unrelievedly harsh from so many quarters? Why do so many good people in schools persist in practicing what they know works poorly? The two of us dared not speak of these things on the way back to the city's center. They were too painful.

After the visit, I tried to answer the question that had taken me there: had Tillson changed since 1981? The response, however tentative, had to be that little had changed in any substantive sense. The school was smaller, but that appeared to have little impact. The compromises of 1981 were still largely there, unaddressed. Only the outside world had significantly changed, and primarily to become ever more hostile to the kinds of young people who attended Tillson High School.

By several general measures, American secondary education, just like Tillson High School, has changed little since 1981. As a result of political pressure on school authorities, students are taking moderately different patterns of courses from earlier ones, concentrating more on the established basic subjects (mathematics, English, science, and social studies) and less on electives with titles such as "Life Skills."[2] This certainly appears to be a change in the right direction, but course titles unfortunately tell us little.[3]

The public schools remain sharply segregated by race and class. For example, the percentage of schoolchildren of color attending schools made up largely of agemates who are not white has grown from 1980 to 1994 despite all the country's efforts at integration. Figures on the concentration of children by income groups are difficult to come by. Suffice it to say that federal programs to aid poor children were concentrated in 1994 much where they were in 1980, a fair indication that the poor in 1994 were in the same places as a decade earlier. The percentage of all school-age children living below the federally assigned poverty line rose from 17.9 percent in 1980 to 21.1 percent in 1992.[4]

Some 76 percent of students in the relevant age group received high school diplomas in 1970. In 1994, the percentage was a bit lower.[5] And then there are test scores, probably the most useful of which are those collected by the federal authorities responsible for the surveys conducted by the National Assessment of Educational Progress. Comparative scoring across a number of secondary school areas reveals little movement.[6] One of the least meaningful but most watched barometers of American schools' success is the College Board's SAT scores. National averages on both the verbal and mathematical parts of the test remain essentially flat, although some improvement was noted in scores arising from testing in the spring of 1995.[7] Certain subgroups within the high school population show improvement, such as those taking the Advanced Placement Examinations offered by the College Board. The courses required to prepare for some of these exams have to be demanding, and the fact that more young people are taking them suggests a trend among some students toward more demanding academic work.[8]

Another revealing barometer of public commitment is school budgets. If we consider spending to be a crude reflection of popular concern, were we allocating more for education in the mid-1990s than in 1980? When we look at the budgets for public elementary and secondary education, we see substantial growth in real dollars. Pulling the data apart, however, reveals that most of that growth is explained by a broadening of programs rather than a deepening of the existing core, by the rapidly increasing expense of "special education" (outlays mandated by federal and state laws), and by raises in teachers' and administrators' salaries (which slumped during the 1970s in real-dollar terms).[9] What we do not see is any growth or deliberately funded alteration in conditions that suggests an interest in changing school routines — the provision of adequate and up-to-date teaching materials and technology, topnotch libraries, school-based professional development, and more.

With all the political rhetoric about the need for reform, why was there so little apparent improvement in the academic performance of high school students over the decade? There are many reasons, but two of the most central leap out of the experience of Tillson High School.

First, the basic routines of the school seemed almost precisely the same in 1981 and 1994 — the rushed schedule, the division of subject matter into unconnected disciplinary specialties, the emphasis on coverage ("Name the principal measures of the New Deal") rather than understanding ("What made the 1930s a likely period for certain kinds of federal social legislation?"), the arranged anonymity of most students (given the way teachers' loads were distributed). Horace's compromises were still very much there. Without change in those routines, which demonstrably served few children well, how could anyone reasonably expect changes — improvements — in the performance of students?

Second, the searing effects of poverty on children worsened. High schools are not social fix-it institutions. If students come to class distracted, hungry, frightened, and believing (with legitimate reason) that the society in which they live neither wants nor cherishes them, it is difficult to bring them to the task of serious, formal academic work.

Where does this schoolbook abstraction lead us? the kids ask. To expect schools to roll back the complex effects of poverty without support is to expect too much.

However, I have seen high schools in similar situations that profoundly reinvented themselves during this period. Why did Tillson not follow a similar track? Perhaps it was because the changes going on in its city — for example, the shrinking of its student body — were too large and too unsettling to allow for concerted educational reform. Perhaps it was because neither Gil nor Sam really put this sort of reform at the top of the agenda. Perhaps there was little interest among or incentive for Tillson's staff to become involved with reform groups across the region or the country. Perhaps the central administration and the city's unions kept a sharp eye out for people who did not adhere to the system's specific rules and expectations, most of which sturdily reinforced the worst as well as the best of the status quo. My hunch is that all of these conditions influenced Tillson's situation.

However, the question remains, what is improvement? Change for change's sake makes no sense. Improved attendance can be a plus — as long as what the students attend to in school is truly worthy of their time. One person's tough course is for another a misguided effort. Better test scores provide a limited and challengeable yardstick, but what sorts of tests are chosen, and what meaning do the scores on them in fact yield?

The past decades' hue and cry over the need for high school reform makes sense. The existing system doesn't work. What is far less clear — and what there should be substantial argument about — is what should replace the schools we have today.

My reflections after my recent visit to Tillson painfully reminded me of how far we need to go in reaching consensus on the goals of education reform. What I (or any one of us) think is an appropriate and rigorous general education for all children — and what it looks like when we see it — is hardly a commonly held and widely accepted viewpoint. A better Tillson for me might well be anathema to another. And some might still like Tillson more or less just as it is, just souped up a bit.

What is surprising is that we Americans rarely argue about this —

about just what sort of school makes sense — in detail. We avoid the crucial particulars. My hunch is that our avoidance is due not so much to lack of interest as to honest confusion. We are uncertain about our basic institutions, including schools. The world is out of joint. How then do we talk of the particularities of schools? How then do we address the mindlessness of the Tillson High Schools of America?

◆ A Place Where Something Happened

During 1983, while I was writing *Horace's Compromise,* I accepted a number of speaking engagements with school people to test my ideas and the directions in which they might lead me. At the conclusion of one such gathering in Massachusetts, I was confronted by a smiling, balding, red-bearded, plaid-shirt–wearing character who bluntly said, "You talk about it. We do it. You better get your butt up to my school."

He was Dennis Littky. I went to his school, Thayer Junior-Senior High School. I found, as he predicted, that he, most of his faculty, and I marched to the same drummer. Thayer was the first school to join the Coalition of Essential Schools.

Thayer Junior-Senior High School, enrolling some 350 students, serves the small, economically struggling, southwestern New Hampshire town of Winchester. In the early 1980s the school was troubled with high truancy and dropout rates, violence, and the indifference and even contempt of most of the community. After a spate of serious disorders, the school committee turned in 1981 to Littky, a new resident, a newspaperman, and, during the 1970s, the founding principal of an award-winning middle school in Shoreham-Wading River on Long Island, New York. He accepted the job, expecting to be given the sweeping freedom necessary to turn the school around.

Before Littky arrived, about a fifth of the students dropped out annually. Today 4 to 6 percent do. Of those who survived until graduation in the early 1980s, some 10 percent went to college. Today the overwhelming majority who start at Thayer graduate, benefiting from the school's commitment to prepare students to pursue the life of their choosing confidently after high school. Some years, as many as two thirds of the graduates continue on to college. The school is proud, orderly, feisty, noticeable, a pride for most of the town, and, in its confident jubilation, a pain for a small minority. It is a school with a pronounced character.

What happened? Littky did several things immediately after his appointment and during the summer before the school year started, thereby creating a momentum and a sense of what did and did not go at Thayer. He got the building and grounds cleaned up. He tried to meet as many of the students personally, informally, as he could. He found a truculent but talented student to paint a mural in the cafeteria. He spent hours meeting townspeople, searching them out in their homes and shops. Thereby he found his friends.

Over just a few years — virtually all at once — he and his faculty made a number of major changes. From the first day of the school year, Littky dealt decisively with disorder. At the same time he devised all sorts of activities to promote the students' pride in their school, largely by assuming that the young people could handle responsibility if it was given to them.

Tracking went; it was assumed that everyone was college bound. The curriculum was narrowed. When Littky arrived, fewer than a quarter of the seniors were taking mathematics. By the mid-1990s, over three quarters were, and comparably rising percentages were seen in the other central academic areas.

Nineteen core skills, such as "distinguishing between evidence and opinion" and "taking measurements in English and metric units and applying them in a variety of practical, scientific, and mathematical ways," were identified and repeatedly stressed, and the school now constantly questions and reevaluates its selection of these core skills. For each student to display mastery of those skills publicly in order to graduate is the school's goal.

The teaching emphasized problem-solving over rote learning, engaging the students in individual and collective work. The teachers taught in grade-level teams, and the school's schedule allowed these teams to meet regularly.

Littky personally prepared the academic schedule for each student, meeting with each one individually each spring. That schedule became a sort of individual contract between the student, the adviser, and the principal. Littky's interest in each young person was obvious.

For potential dropouts, a special integrated program was developed. It involved these students deeply in community work, such as building a post-and-beam house using some of the technologies of an earlier era, and was supervised by a teacher-artisan who had a special knack with the often sullen and angry kids who found their way into his program.

Students connected academic work with matters in the town — elections, the toxicity of the local dump, and the operation of shops, for example — and those responsible for these enterprises were included in the school's agenda.

None of these moves were new in the school world, although they were new for Thayer. However, we can learn special lessons from Thayer High School's experience.

The school was small. The principal could quickly get to know his students, their families, and the faculty, thereby creating the possibility of a coherent community with the ability to deal with its issues honestly. People could rely on each other. Relationships were possible.

The tone of the school, from the first day, was respectful. Littky was criticized for this, as respect for a troubled or misguided teenager was often deemed by impatient and threatened adults to be unwarranted. The feel of the school was informal; adults and students easily related to each other. Some critics found this informality a sign of disrespect, but given the deliberate family-like culture of this school, the opposite was the case.

Students carried substantial responsibilities — for example, for acting as mentors to the ninth-graders, for meeting and briefing visitors, for running the "back room" of the elaborate interactive national television show that the school created in the early 1990s *(Here, Thayer, Everywhere)*.

For several years Littky gave each of his teachers a bound blank notebook at the start of the school year. He encouraged them to write him a letter in it every Wednesday, and he replied in every notebook. An atmosphere of interest in the students was built within the faculty, and the students showed its effects.

The changes were clear, persuasive, and bold, and where they interconnected, they were launched simultaneously. This drew charges of "too much change too quickly." Thayer's experience, however, reinforces the point that schools are complex, interrelated entities and that change of any consequence has to reflect this. Tepid change is no change at all, or worse, if it corrodes the energy of the risk-takers.

Thayer and Littky had extraordinary freedom to make the changes they desired, and they could act with dispatch. No one expected to have to ask for permission. Ironically, New Hampshire, well known for its puny support of public education, resolutely acts by its motto, "Live free or die," in the sense that there is little tight state regulation and not much supervision of what little there is. This gives great freedom to an entrepreneur such as Littky (as well as to sleepy principals who do nothing, alas, to improve their schools). Littky's superintendent, Richard McCarthy, was a patient behind-the-scenes supporter throughout, dealing as required with the political snags Littky encountered.

In due course Littky and his school encountered serious political troubles, ones driven by a small but well-organized minority of citizens. Twice the school committee fired him (for no clearly stated reasons, but probably because of his independent and informal ways); twice he withstood the firing by appealing to the courts and then to the state board of education. Under pressure, Littky did not quit, and his backers ultimately overcame the opposition by electing a supportive school board by a substantial margin. When Littky resigned in 1994, the political channels were happily clear.

The school continues to flourish. Littky's successor, Jed Butterfield, describes part of his task wisely by asking, how can a small school so richly infused with the energy and direction of a charismatic leader continue to grow and to serve its youngsters well after that popular figure leaves?

Thayer's experience raises a general question, too: does all reform depend on such a leader? To my eye, there are clear lessons from the recent history of that high school that go beyond the person of Dennis

Littky. The merit of small schools; the need to invest time in connections and relationships within the school and its community; the wisdom of a sharp, clear focus for the academic program, insistence on the formal public display of student work, and high expectations for all students; and the necessity of stable leadership for more than a decade all seem crucial.

But outstanding leadership is necessary, clearly, to break the dam of inertia that affects most American high schools. That is a shame; it should not have to be so. Sensible reform should not be so hard.

Dennis Littky is currently a senior fellow at the Annenberg Institute for School Reform at Brown University and codirector of Big Picture Inc., a not-for-profit school reform organization in Rhode Island. He was New Hampshire Principal of the Year in 1992. Thayer High School's saga under his leadership is recorded in a book, DOC *(Chicago: Contemporary Books, 1989), and a film produced by NBC,* A Town Torn Apart. *In 1994,* Here, Thayer, Everywhere, *the school initiated countrywide interactive television program for teachers and students, won an Innovations in State and Local Government Award, sponsored by the Ford Foundation and the John F. Kennedy School of Government at Harvard University.*

Thayer Junior-Senior High School, Winchester, New Hampshire; James Butterfield, principal. Member of the Coalition of Essential Schools since 1984.

2

There Is More to It
than Just the Schools

EVEN THOUGH they are quite alike in many respects, Tillson and Thayer High Schools serve their students profoundly differently. Neither is perfect. Neither will be as effective or ineffective tomorrow as they are today. Both are served by decent and hard-working adults. The majority of students in each come from low-income families. Both reside in economically hard-hit communities.

Thayer, however, is a small school. It is set in a coherent, rural community. The kids are well known. There is no need, therefore, for metal detectors and the mistrust they symbolize. Straying youngsters are quickly found by their advisers. People rather than a computer system keep track of the kids. Thayer is attuned to its students. They are recognized as individuals, the most compelling form of respect. Accordingly, most of them show up at school most of the time. A goodly number work hard while there.

The faculty is small enough to find within itself a sense of community. That faculty and the principal have extraordinary freedom to shape their school in ways that they and their greater community want, rather than to march to a standardized system developed elsewhere. This allows them, as a result, to narrow their work to essentials, to run a school so simple in its construction that it can readily bend to the needs of particular children, to design a school that fits into the economy and concerns of its town. The freedom they have and the accountability that that freedom carries with it serve as an elixir.

Thayer's community had the intelligence to appoint a brilliant principal and the political stuffing to stand by him when he and his staff made the wrenching changes in the school that conditions required.

It is possible to change schools for the better. It is difficult to do so, especially when the students arrive at the school's door with the terrors and scars of poverty. The irony is that schools serving America's poor usually end up with fewer uncommitted dollars to deploy to their students' requirements than schools in more affluent districts.

However, the educational damage wreaked by America's current careless culture is not limited to places where poor folks live. In 1994 I spent a day at Carney Middle School, in an affluent suburban district. The expansive one-story building was set on a large plot, with playing fields extending grandly off in one direction and woods in another. It was a happy place; laughter and easy banter were the rule. Some youngsters enrolled there came from the inner city, and Asian American families were moving in; the hallways were not monochromatically Caucasian, as they had been only a few years earlier. The faculty was as feisty as it was veteran. Teachers who come to work at this school never leave.

At the end of the day, I listened to Carney's principal and teachers. They were excited and realistic about the changes they were making, both in their expectations for their students and in their daily routines. They saw progress, and while it was slower in coming than they had hoped, they were convinced that they were on the right track. The students had more focused academic work; more questions were posed to them, and they were given fewer canned answers to memorize. Their work was presented publicly (the Coalition calls these projects Exhibitions) for the community to see.

Only bit by bit did the faculty tell stories that conveyed a darker tale about these students. A third of their fathers were out of work, according to the principal's careful guess. The town was heavily dependent on three high-tech industries, and, starting in 1990, two had taken huge financial hits. The third was a major defense contractor that was downsizing precipitously. All three were restructuring — an expression applied to a staggering business, and another of the grim code words for layoffs. The Plymouth Voyagers and BMWs still drove up to school, parents were publicly cheery, but instability was the sudden reality for many of these affluent families. The fact that the mothers might be working too, and at professionals' salaries, steadied some of them, but the loss was inescapable. Indeed, maybe there was only one parent to begin with. The situation told on the kids, the teachers said. The youngsters were often distracted.

It was winter, and we talked of snow days. Snow or no snow, some children, it seemed, were always dropped off at school. Therefore, the principal said, she and some teachers always had to be there, no matter what instructions had gone out over the radio in the morning. Some families had no backup child care at all, no extended families or open-armed neighbors to lend a hand or a safe living room. Such parents simply left the children at the curb in front of the school. And even on snow-free days, a teacher or two always hung around late for children who did not take scheduled buses and who were not picked up by someone on time, or at all. These youngsters were often frightened and needed help. They had to know that they had not been forgotten. All this attention was not technically within the school's obligations, but the faculty accepted the responsibilities on moral grounds, or so the principal implied.

A counselor told of the increasing challenge he found in his work. "What used to happen to tenth-graders now is routine among eighth-graders," he said. Trouble with the law. Promiscuity. Pregnancy. Parties with alcohol and without adults in attendance. Drugs. Abuse. But behind this, surely, was the youngsters' sense of being on their own, by default masters of their fate. *Home Alone* was more than just a movie for them, and perhaps the media, full of stories of teenagers on their own, taught them that this was the way life is. There were no gangs yet in this fashionable town, but in one form or another they would come, providing ways for young people to find the kind of protection they felt they needed.[1] The counselor shrugged his shoulders. It is all so hard, he finally said.

As I left the school building to go home, I saw in a new way all these bright and eager and noisy children, now waiting for buses or for some after-school activity. Given their surface wholesomeness, it was difficult to calculate the strain in many of their lives. These bouncy, colorful kids put flesh and blood on the oft-cited statistics about America's youth and how we Americans nurture or neglect them. That they were largely the children of American affluence made the message especially powerful. It is not only among the poor that anxiety and abuse and inattention thrive. And the strain affects the parents too. It shows.

The story of the new American poverty has been repeatedly told over the past few years. A fifth of our children are growing up in poverty (defined by the federal government in 1992 as an annual income of $14,335 or less for a family of four, itself an astonishingly low figure).[2] The majority of these families are led by a mother alone.[3] Over half a million babies are born to teenagers each year, four fifths to unmarried women.[4]

For many American young people, school is the last, best sanctuary, the one place, as one inner-city technical high school principal told me, where a student can trust that an adult is concerned for him or her. Home and street are uncertain places. Upwards of 9 million adolescents have no health-care coverage.[5] No other age group is subject to higher rates of physical violence, often inflicted on each other.[6] America's adolescents are on their own in a way we have not seen for eighty years.

But the problems do not sharply decline as family income goes up. Carney Middle School is not the exception. The stresses within American communities are substantial, and the effects on children are demonstrable but difficult to reduce to the kinds of statistics on which governments depend. How do we calculate the strain on a family when its wage-earners fear that they may precipitously lose their jobs? How do we measure the costs paid by the latchkey child, or by the parents for being forced to give that latchkey to their child?

It is not that America is poor. We remain the richest country in the history of the world. We choose, however, to spend our money on our private lives and not on our communities. Those who have some money are given the means to get more of it, and those who don't have an ever harder struggle to catch up. The result is the emergence of two Americas, one rich and one poor. The existence of these two Americas defines us, expresses our values, defines our collective character. It is the great American embarrassment.

To forward the reform of schools — the society's one remaining collective universal venture — is fiercely difficult. On one hand, the children are ever needier. On the other, government is both confused by the economic mess that it perceives itself to be entangled in and unwilling to extend a secure and sufficient safety net to all its young citizens. School people, parents, and the children are left in the middle, periodically exhorted by the political powers that be to reform themselves and in many communities left with few resources to address the incontestably real conditions that scream for reform.

Schools are to raise their standards. Fine; Horace agrees. Who can be against that? But what about standards of decency and assistance for young citizens in need? The children did not ask to be born. They have broken no law. What about standards for a system that accelerates the inequity in which they live? Who will test for that?

I was amused recently to watch my grandchildren exchanging e-mail addresses with their cousins. Eight-year-olds jabbering on computers, poking into the Internet, playing mindful and mindless games: it is a new world. Their grandfather was raised with daily newspapers, *Life* magazine, the radio, and the Victrola. The explosion of influences on today's children has no precedent.

MTV is only fifteen years old. CNN dates from 1980, and C-Span began broadcasting in 1979. Only a few households had VCRs in 1980. The first CD-ROM encyclopedia was marketed by Grolier in 1987. The television set is turned on some seven hours a day in the typical American household. America's population is awash in information, on a scale exponentially greater than anything that has come before.

The media revolution has profound effects on schooling. It sets an agenda; it tells kids from Seattle to Savannah what is good or bad, funny or dull, in or out. Above all, it markets goods. At its best it is vivid and immediate: tanks firing on Iraqis in Kuwait, the O.J. Simpson trial, the crowds staggering away from the Oklahoma City bombing, the extraordinarily orchestrated exhibitions of rock video, the fun of instant letter writing, the magic of the Internet, the cleverness of a game, the wonders of a new art form, like that displayed in *Toy Story*. At worst it is an enormous distraction and an appeal to the unintellectual. It wants to do the thinking and the feeling for the watcher. At best it is the opening to a new and richer culture, one that has instant global reach and enormous flexibility. Given its scale, ultimate low cost, and accessibility, it promises a great deal for democracy.

The implications for high school are profound. Horace sees it in his classes. Today's students know different things from their predecessors. The imagination has more equipment in its arsenal. Before, there was language alone; now there is language and color and movement and sound, accessible to the youngest budding artist. Before, there was a textbook with illustrations; now there is video as well. Before, there was science laboratory equipment; now there are computer simulations of experiments in "laboratories" beyond the wildest dreams of the teachers of a generation ago.

Earlier, what went home from school was the book and the tablet of blank paper. Now the full reach of the Internet is added to that — in the living room. Given this power, some kids ask, why go to school so much? Indeed, replies Horace. How must schools change to seize the best of this extraordinary new power? The same old stuff, however well it worked before, often seems thin to Horace now. The students are impatient with a curriculum reflecting past (and thus limited) access to information and tools that pre-date the computer. The influences from the outside world are far more insistent on them than they were on adolescents even twenty years ago.

Technology is no panacea, any more than the 180-day school year is a panacea. Nonetheless, the new technologies have already changed the ways in which adolescents get information and attitudes. Further, their potential for serious education is immense. Given that, Horace knows, there must be a profound rethinking of the purposes and functioning of the Franklin High Schools and a public decision about all people's right to use these powerful systems. Some grandfathers have grandchildren with no access to computers, and no incentive from parents to get that access.

Tillson, Thayer, and Carney are all schools in transition. American culture is in the midst of extraordinary change. Much now seems rootless, and educators control a shrinking fraction of the attention of adolescents and their communities. Reform is therefore frustratingly complicated. Much of what contemporary authorities demand of schools consists of imperatives from an earlier time, the toughening up of old routines. Horace senses that this is not enough, is an incomplete response, even a retrogressive response.

Horace wishes for some persuasive cultural hitching posts, even a fresh and decisive guiding star. Without such a star, reform easily descends into a numbing process of rearranging the familiar and hectoring young people to do things that fail to make much sense. Horace knows that this will not work, however insistent the rhetoric behind it is. What the typical good school now purveys does not work, at least not well enough. However, just what is to replace it is not evident.

There is frustration here, and dismay over the country's inability to face up to its ills. However, Horace also knows there is promise in this culturally and politically fluid moment in American history.

✦ Massive Middle Schools

Good large middle schools are an oxymoron. Managers who in the name of efficiency pack hundreds of awkward, often frightened preteens into massive buildings forget what a crowd means to an eleven-year-old, particularly if most of the other people there, both kids and adults, are total strangers and often speak a different language. Efficiency, one wonders, of what sort and for whom?

Lincoln Middle School in Santa Monica and O'Farrell Community School in San Diego, both in California, are big schools. Lincoln enrolls over 1000 children, and O'Farrell 1400. Both serve diverse populations. Lincoln's youngsters, for example, arrive from households in which twenty-seven different languages are spoken. Over a third of these children and over two thirds of O'Farrell's children come from low-income homes. The transience of their families is high. Thirteen percent of the children who register at Lincoln in the fall will have moved away by the following June.

The very existence of schools this large sends a confusing message to their faculties and the children's parents. Bigness all too readily signals a need for order — crowd control, some call it — and order all too usually implies standardized routines and a rule-driven, impersonal school culture.

In the face of disorder and stress in their lives — at home, on the street, responding to the media — young adolescents need order in their school. They need much more than this, however, including sensitivity of a particular sort — sensitivity that recognizes and respects the extraordinary physical and emotional changes that most of them are experiencing. Early adolescence is not called the awkward age for nothing.

In the late 1980s, the middle-school years became the subject of a variety of inquiries, the most influential of which was the Task Force on Education of Young Adolescents, sponsored by the Carnegie Corporation of New York. The report issued by the Carnegie panel in 1989, *Turning Points: Preparing American Youth for the 21st Century,* came to similar conclusions on many grounds as our Study of High Schools.[7] Californian educators took a further step by appointing a state commission on middle schools, which issued its own report. Again the recommendations were congruent with the ideas emerging from the work of the Coalition. The reform efforts were clearly on parallel paths.

Lincoln and O'Farrell, both members of the Coalition of Essential Schools since 1991, took similar steps to relieve the impersonality (and other problems) of the big buildings they had been dealt — steps that reflected Essential Schools' ideas and those of Carnegie and the state.

Both broke their schools into smaller units: O'Farrell into "families" of 6 faculty members and 160 seventh- and eighth-graders, and 3 faculty members and 75 sixth-graders; Lincoln into core teams of 4 to 5 teachers with 100 to 175 students.

Both encouraged interdisciplinary work within these small units, in effect creating small schools. The teams had substantial blocks of time at their disposal and arranged their schedules to serve their particular youngsters best.

Both drove their curricula with questions such as Lincoln's "Whose water is this, anyway?" which focused on California water resources and the use of and claims to that water by various groups. O'Farrell connected the past with the present, considering the experiences of Gandhi and Martin Luther King, Jr., as they might relate to the 1992 riots in south-central Los Angeles.

O'Farrell articulated the "O'Farrell Standard," a list of challenges that students had to accomplish in an effective manner; for example, "twelve hours of community service . . . a sustained research project that explores a real-life problem . . . competence leading to a college-prep high school level in self-expression, academic reading, mathematical reasoning."

Small units. Students known well by a team of teachers. A focused program. A school day broken into large blocks of time for each team's use. A curriculum driven by questions that force the students to engage their minds. Regular, formal Exhibitions by the students. Careful attention to the culture of the schools: high expectations, service to the community, attention to morale.

None is a radical idea. All have been suggested by several reform initiatives. All have affected the performance of students at O'Farrell and Lincoln.

O'Farrell graduates are taking higher-level mathematics courses in high school than either their predecessors or the alumni of other San Diego middle schools. Test scores of incoming O'Farrell students are below the national median. When they graduate, the same youngsters score above the comparable median on six of nine subtests. Disciplinary problems, previously a major problem, have sharply declined. Daily attendance is 95 percent and teacher turnover is below 10 percent — both strikingly favorable for a school of this kind.

From 1990 to 1993, the percentage of Lincoln students who scored in the high honors or honors range in the Golden State algebra examination rose from 39 to 81. On the new (and now discontinued) performance-based assessment tests administered in 1993, 68 percent of Lincoln students received the highest rubric scores of 6, 5, or 4 on normed writing tests, compared to 42 percent statewide; 53 percent received rubric scores of 6, 5, or 4 on normed reading tests, compared to 39 percent statewide; and 23 percent received rubric scores of 6, 5, or 4 on normed mathematics tests, compared to 11 percent statewide.

These indices provide only one sort of evidence. Visitors to these large schools sense another — that these are not factories, that the children like being there and by the lights of early adolescents they work hard, that the buildings are accurately perceived to be safe places, that the faculties are pulling together and share pride in their work.

The lessons are familiar.

Massive schools make no sense. They are profoundly inefficient.

Human-scale places are a necessary precondition for serious academic work, especially by young adolescents. It is possible to create human-scale places inside big buildings.

Children, like all of us, learn best in familiar settings that they perceive to be both safe and led by teachers who really know them.

Collective work — the development of common standards, for example — energizes a faculty, even though its members may disagree from time to time. Such work brings respect and common focus.

Children, even those from stress-filled homes (the frequently inevitable consequence of poverty) or those who speak a language other than English or those who have recently arrived from a strikingly different culture, will come to class, work together, achieve and sustain some sort of worthy hope — if the school is receptive, respectful, flexible, and responsive.

Reform is easier when it draws sustenance and authority from several quarters: in the cases of O'Farrell and Lincoln, from the district superintendents, from the Coalition of Essential Schools, from the Carnegie middle schools initiative, from the California SB 1274 School Restructuring Efforts, from the reinforcing activities of the state department of education.

Stable leadership is essential. Both schools' principals have stayed the course, and they and their faculties have played important roles in regional, state, and national reform activity, bringing their experience to the larger discussion and borrowing the best from colleagues beyond their communities.

Lincoln Middle School, Santa Monica, California; Ilene Straus, principal. Member of the Coalition of Essential Schools since 1991. O'Farrell Community School, San Diego, California; Robert Stein, chief education officer. Member of the Coalition of Essential Schools since 1991.

3

The Words of Reform

IF HORACE REQUIRES a new and persuasive reform star by which he can guide his school, he may find the first indications of it in the language of the current debate about American schooling, particularly in the slogans emerging in discussions of educational policy. Eight words or phrases have been the special workhorses of the school reform discussion for more than a decade:

All children can learn
Accountability
Choice
Public education
A nation at risk
World-class standards
Systemic reform
Multiculturalism

For some, these words have become mantras. In others they trigger almost visceral opposition. Because of their overuse, they are frequently treated with scorn. Without question, however, they represent flashpoints for educational policy and practice. Most important, they chart an emerging way, a direction for Horace.

All children can learn

Of course they can and do and always have. The point of this platitude, however, is to signal the expectation that schools will function on that assumption. Bluntly, if a child does not learn, we must blame his school, not him.

This represents a major and desirable switch in responsibility. In the past, if a youngster did not "get it," he was identified as more or less incompetent and put in an "appropriate" program or track, one that had simpler, less demanding criteria for success. The conventional way to identify the "getting" of "it" — that is, to show evidence that the student has learned what the teacher wanted learned — is usually a standardized procedure to which all students are exposed. It is expected, indeed planned for, that some youngsters will fail on these tests. Traditionally, schools have sorted kids out.

The new assumption, which has emerged in the past fifteen years, is that if a kid does not get it in the usual way, the school should try to help him to get it in another way. Everybody has to get it. No one can be sorted out. The stakes are high, not only for the individual youngster but also for the rest of us, who will have to support citizens who cannot hack it in a complex economy and society.

Some argue the "all children can learn" principle on the basis of changes in the labor market. A strong back attached to a poorly educated mind worked in an industrial age, but it will not work in an information age. Some argue, as several of the Founding Fathers pronounced, that democracy depends on a truly informed citizenry and that schools should prepare everyone, without exception, for civic duty. In our complex society, brute literacy and numeracy no longer will suffice. Still others argue that the standardized system of education is unfair, rewarding only some students and misclassifying and misteaching others. We fail to identify and thus to use the talents of many children, this argument goes, and we cruelly humiliate good young people by giving up on them for specious reasons. Finally, some argue that every person deserves to get it — to learn well — as a simple right. People who are not prepared to use their minds and hearts in meaningful ways miss out on a rich life. A worthy, generous society provides for the getting of it.

Much depends, of course, on just how "it" is defined. For those for whom "all children can learn" is a settled principle, that definition is a detail, albeit an important one. For them, the commitment to learning for all (not just access to schooling for all) is the necessary point of departure, whether or not every child is able to use calculus or speak at least two languages or leave school prepared to enter college or take a serious job or have a working grasp of the details of democratic government (or of a moral society) and the conviction and respect to use them.

Critics reasonably complain that the schools cannot be expected to carry such a load alone and that influences beyond their doors count for much or most of a child's world, particularly his interest in studying hard at school. Some critics challenge the entire proposition. Who are we adults to tell an adolescent that he must learn what we want him to learn?[1] Supporters of the concept reply that schools must connect powerfully with their students' families and the community in which they reside, making all involved in each child's life fully committed allies on behalf of that child. A school cannot be an island, they argue. Learning for all children demonstrably requires the determined collaboration of all the key figures in each child's life. They must persuade him. However, the school, they argue, should take the initiative in making this happen.

"All children can learn" raises the stakes for schools in a persuasive, desirable, and long overdue way.

Accountability

Of course schools must be accountable. They always have been, in one way or another. For generations there has been direction and oversight by local school boards and state boards of education as well as by representatives of the traditional administrative bureaucracies.

The current use of the word "accountability," however, is code for an unequivocal conclusion that today's schools are not succeeding. The assumption is that if they were *really* held accountable, they would clean up their act. Imbedded in this assumption is the idea that the existing apparatus of accountability either does not work or cannot work, an idea that rose and gained momentum in the late 1960s.

The key question is, accountable to whom? Few of the most vocal demanders of accountability call on local school boards or on the officials in the education bureaucracies in these matters. Indeed, the dismissal of these traditional agencies for management and oversight of schools is sweeping. The two new centers of authority are the state governments and the consumers themselves, principally parents. The shadows cast by each of these, however, fall in strikingly different directions.

On one hand, many states, exercising their constitutional obligation to provide for public schools, have drawn the reins of control ever tighter, largely through legislation setting out new mandates (for example, requiring four years of English in high school) and through elaborate testing programs. Some of these tests are intended to be for "high stakes," meaning that failure will cut off opportunity. That is, they are not to be used merely to inform teachers and parents; they carry important social consequences. If students fail repeatedly, the state will bring direct sanctions against their school. If they do well, there will be rewards, for them and their teachers. The scores from these tests might even be made public, in the hope that humiliation will provoke remedial action.[2]

On the other hand, some prominent critics contend that accountability most appropriately rests with the consumers: the children and their families. They are the ones who should set the standards, this argument goes, and they are the ones who should decide whether these standards are met. It is all right for the state and the professionals to suggest — indeed, vigorously to argue for — a certain quality and kind of education, but it is not for them finally to control the manner and consequences of the schooling that each student ultimately elects. Children's minds and hearts are family business. Free thought is a bedrock of democracy, and state-controlled education challenges that condition. Detailed state control, some argue, is at root totalitarian.[3]

To confuse matters, both these voices sometimes appear to be singing the same song. Periodically the tunes tend toward harmony, with the state asserting that it will insist only on setting the general goals and standards for education and on assessing each student's progress toward meeting those standards. All the rest of keeping school is to be left to the locals. Many think this arrangement is a hoax. They hotly protest that standards and assessments are the heart of education and that the rest is detail. The harmony, they argue, masks the continued primary authority of the state.

As before, behind all this remains the question of just what "it" is for which children and schools will be held accountable. Clarity on that point inevitably alters reactions to which accountability applies to whom and in what form.

The fact remains that those most involved in the debate over public education appear to agree that the local and state boards of education and the administrators who work for them, long entrusted with account-ability, do not serve that function well. Accountability is necessary, all agree. A new, better system has to be created. In that creation, the issues of *accountable to whom* and *accountable for what* will be nicely and appropriately embedded. A wise resolution will require a new balance of authority between families and government, with a significant tilt toward the former, and a respectful acknowledgment and accommoda-tion of the diversity within our society.

Choice

Of course. Families should be able to pick which schools their children will attend. No law denies this right. Private schools are constitutionally protected and serve their customers in meeting the requirements of state compulsory education laws.

Or so it is in theory. Choice of a child's school has always been an option for wealthier parents, for families that have the financial strength and stability to move into a community where there are "desirable" schools or to pay tuition for their child's enrollment at a private school. Suburban public schools have long been a magnet for their communi-ties. Good schools mean higher real estate values. The choice that wealthier Americans have long enjoyed explains why so many public school systems are so sharply segregated by social class and thus to a considerable extent by race and ethnicity. The Americans without choice are the poor or those of particular racial or ethnic origin who in subtle or unsubtle ways are denied admission to communities of their liking.

Some proponents of educational choice seek to redress this wrong, arguing that if school attendance is compulsory and that if some parents have the freedom to select the site of their child's compulsory attendance, then everyone should have that right, not only before the law but in reality. For a quarter-century such proponents have pursued this goal, but only those remedies associated with segregation by race — remedies following the 1954 *Brown* decision — have had much force.[4] Most Americans want choice; or, more accurately, they do not — at least in theory — want government telling them where their children will be schooled, any more than they would tolerate government's telling them where to live. In practice, for most youngsters the school down the street is the school of choice (as the family has decided to live near it), and many parents are more or less at peace with this fact, particularly because community-organized schools tend to be homogeneous places. Heated arguments about school assignment are most often found in places that are demographically diverse or tenanted by substantial numbers of low-income families.

Some want choice so they can send their children to schools with curricula and cultures at odds with those accepted by the mainstream public schools — schools, for example, that stress very traditional subject matter, or that are single-sex, or that place substantial freedom in the hands of their students, or that practice highly tuned forms of democratic governance, with parents involved in all the immediate decisions, or that stress certain religious, ethical, or social values. Others want choice not so much to provide an education out of the mainstream as to conduct education in what they believe is a better and more efficient way. That is, they do not disagree with their local public school's goals as much as with how that school is organized to meet them.

The disagreements among these groups are substantial. In much of the public debate over choice, these differences have remained blurred. Choice advocates therefore appear to be a collection of the most unlikely bedfellows. Some are citizens who desire a particular focus and intensity in the schools for their own children, and who think it unlikely that such a disciplined school will emerge within the present system. Others are urban school reformers, many of whom align themselves with the political left, who are designing small "alternative" schools nestled within the big districts. There are home-school advocates, who defy consistent political assignment and who want substantial and direct control over the schooling of their children. There are system reformers, usually political conservatives, who believe that choice will create a market among schools that will break what they perceive to be a rigid and regressive public school monopoly. There are citizens who want public aid to be brought in some constitutional way to both nonsectarian and sectarian religious schools. There are school boards and administrators who want to lessen tension in their school systems by allowing parents to have significant options for the children.

This fascinating and politically diverse cacophony reflects the growing — and sensible — acceptance of the notion that schools should not necessarily be alike and that families should have far greater control over the particular schools that their children attend than they have had. Choice is on the banners of many influential groups. It is now a deeply entrenched idea. The day of a one best system designed by experts for the mandatory use of all appears, mercifully, to have passed.[5]

Public education

The two words slip easily off our tongues. What, however, is meant by *public,* especially in a world of choice among schools?

Several definitions are generally acknowledged. Public means that every child attends. All the people pay the schools' bills, out of tax revenues. Everyone has a hand in the control of education. Government is usually expected to run the schools rather than, for example, contracting out their functioning. Everyone has the right to attend. Access is guaranteed.

In some quarters today, the word *public* provokes a snarl. If the schools are publicly run, this conventional wisdom has it, they will be inefficient or replete with patronage and strangled by politics. Privatization is better. The marketplace is better. Public management means monopoly and monopolies are bad.

The questions of control and the locus of funding the schools (state, local, or federal) are fully heard in the current debate over schooling. However, the issue of access is not, and the gap is a serious one — public education's dirtiest little secret. Access to the schools is sharply restricted by custom and law. One goes to a school in one's district. One cannot go to a school outside of one's district. This is the rule, made stark by some interesting and relatively recent exceptions, such as the cross-district enrollment schemes launched over the past decade in Minnesota.

Public transport has total access. I can board a bus or train in South Chicago and go to Lake Forest, and vice versa. I can lawfully mingle in each place with whomever I want. Most other publicly financed enterprises function likewise. I can go to Yosemite National Park whether I live in Harlem or Scarsdale. I can be called to military duty whether I live in Compton or Beverly Hills. I stand in the line at the Registry of Motor Vehicles in my elegant mink or in my oversized, soiled Raiders parka. I can vote, wherever I may live.

However, I cannot go to any public school, whatever my merits, or at least to most schools in the greater metropolitan areas. If I live in Compton, I go to Compton's schools. If I live in Lake Forest, I go to Lake Forest's schools. The so-called public schools are selectively open to all. Access is restricted by residence.

Not surprisingly, there are profound differences between the schools serving poor communities and those serving rich communities. And the fact that influential leaders who live in wealthier communities have to welcome only their own kinds of children into their particular schools profoundly affects the public policy they push forward. The improvement of schools for all is not their most personally compelling priority.

An irony is that some private schools in metropolitan communities, notably those operated by the Roman Catholic Church, serve more economically and racially diverse student bodies than many of the public schools in their regions do. Along the axis of access, which of these schools are more truly public?

As the debate currently swirls around the idea of choice and the virtues of privatization (by which is meant the nonpublic operation of schools at the public's general expense), the question of access is barely heard. The compartmentalization of America, with people gathered with their economic or racial or ethnic kind and protective of the specialness of their turf, does not square with the classic American hope for public education as a place where all Americans meet and become Americans, or even with the expectation that a family can choose any school for its children. In most schools, we are content to present the glories of this one-country-together Americanism at arm's length, safely within the abstractions of the curriculum, ignoring the fact that this curriculum will be taught in "public" schools that are dramatically segregated — a segregation that is sanctioned by law.

Most public education is not truly public at all, and that fact has nothing to do with the competence or incompetence of public management. It arises from the geographic restrictions within which most school systems operate. A policy of choice among public schools by definition creates another kind of segregation: only families who want their children to be at a particular school will be represented there. However, if any family, irrespective of its residence, has fair access to any school — can choose any school — then the basis for segregation is benign. No one should be categorically denied access to any public school. This should be the goal of public policy. This is truly *public* education.

A nation at risk

This phrase arrived on the political scene as the lead image in a report by the National Commission on Excellence in Education issued in 1983, during the first Reagan years. "If an unfriendly foreign power had attempted to impose on America the mediocre educational performance that exists today, we might well have viewed it as an act of war," the report's commissioners asserted.[6] Such purple rhetoric caught the public's attention, and a great deal of churning around, largely in state capitals, ensued.

The 1983 commission not only raised the decibel level of criticism, it made the problem *national.* The commissioners believed that the problem required a systematic countrywide response. The "enemy" was not a foreign army but foreign economic competition. If Americans did not get their educational act together, the commissioners argued, the nation would not have the intellectually supple workforce necessary to compete globally, and the schools had to be marshaled toward that national purpose.

During the 1980s, rhetorical deference was paid to the local character of public education, but in reality state authorities took assertive leadership. The assumption that the states would work in concert with the federal government in an overall educational strategy sank deep roots. By the Bush and Clinton administrations — and there was remarkably little difference in educational policies between them — the national government was tacitly expected to take a major and unprecedented role in association with the states in directing education. The rhetoric was very masculine, reminiscent of military sloganeering, full of calls for toughening up, for rigor, for high standards, for excellence.

The Clinton administration's Goals 2000 legislation, passed by the 103rd Congress, provided the beginnings of a national framework for public education. The arrival in January 1995 of the 104th Congress, dominated by Republicans, caused a pause in this development. The Republican leaders knew, it seemed, what they did not like but were not clear about what they would provide in its place. The assumption that the United States needs some sort of national policy for elementary and secondary education, however, was not likely to disappear. The national school system could no longer be merely the sum of all the state and local efforts. Something more rational was needed.

The clash between a national system and the idea of choice is a deep and obvious one, not yet fully joined. Further, the notion that a national school system must by definition be governmentally directed begs challenge. This is not the case in higher education, so why with the schools? A system of schools that arises from local imperatives, many believe, is more likely to serve this nation well than a system imposed in its most important respects from the political center.

World-class standards

Good schools have clear goals and a worthy standard that each student must reach. Bad schools count any sort of work that appears marginally to represent a student's "coverage" of some material.

Too many American schools have sloppy goals and rubbery standards. Many educators and political leaders therefore believe that this is where reform must start — in the setting of goals and in the demarcation of high standards for their achievement. This is the argument for what is now termed "standards-driven reform," yet another offshoot of the 1983 *A Nation at Risk* report, one eagerly seized by state governments ever since. The Coalition of Essential Schools' advocacy of Exhibitions exemplifies this general point of view. There is widespread and sensible support for this strategy, and tens of millions of dollars have been poured into it, more than any other sort of school reform approach has received.[7]

The trick, as always, lies in the definitions and details. The oft-used and pretentious qualifier "world-class" highlights the problem. It implies both that somewhere out there on the globe is a Standard that is preeminent and that such a high intellectual summit can be defined with the precision and assurance of the timing of the best mile-long footrace ever. In the world of the mind, however, things are not so simple, and the reduction of the standards argument to an image of some sort of fixed world-class standard demeans and undermines the approach.

The problems are obvious. The most vexing questions lie beyond rudimentary issues such as whether the child can read and whether the child can cipher. What does the display of high-quality work include? Is it the expression at a given moment — a testing situation, perhaps — of certain facts and skills? Or is it estimable quality in the use of those facts and skills in some unfamiliar situation? Or is it evidence that the mastery of those facts and skills and their resourceful use has become a matter of habit for the young person?

Unfortunately, most current representations of "world-class" effort meeting a high standard comprise only the first and sometimes the second category. The third is ignored, even though the development of powerful intellectual habits is what most people agree schools are for. Knowing stuff is nice. Being able to use that stuff makes sense. Being disposed to use it always, as a matter of habit, is the brass ring, the ultimate standard. If that demand is never made, then students will never work at it and are thus unlikely to learn it.

In current discussion, this line of argument is rarely followed to its logical conclusion, largely because some people want to reduce evidence of world-class standards to immediate scores on inexpensive tests — and habits are extremely difficult to score. Paradoxically, then, we accept low-quality criteria to define high-quality work.

There is more. Beyond the obvious rudiments, are there universal standards? Or will responsible scholars continually disagree? Can all standards be readily assessed? For example, are there measurable standards for the creation of subtle and powerful works of art or approaches to a complex mathematical proof? Might there be, therefore, significantly different standards for the same sort of work, and if so, which is "world-class"? If the assessment of some important matters cannot be reduced to objective measures that can be universally applied, what then?

The problems continue. Who sets these standards, and by what right? The scholarly community? The state? The teachers in a school? Each child's parents? A grand assembly of all the above, coming to some sort of collective compromise? Or is such a compromise both impossible and unwise, given the happy inevitability of scholarly and ideological disagreements?

From Frederick's Prussia to the modern Soviet Union, certain states have set out a specific educational program and held their people to it. The results, both of the political abuse of such an approach and of the stubbornness of the human spirit in rejecting it, are before us. Current American attempts to have national standards that are even loosely aligned with national assessments and curricula (even if called "voluntary" — money follows only those who opt in) are heading down a dangerous and potentially undemocratic road. Those who say that censorship and ideologically dominated curricula cannot happen here can find it everywhere today, albeit mostly at local levels. Some recent American culture wars, such as that over multiculturalism, reveal a frantic ferocity. To try to create some sort of imposed national educational pattern is as imprudent politically as it is unwise as a matter of scholarship and democratic philosophy.

High-quality intellectual work cannot be bottled. Scholarship — and it is scholarship that we must expect of secondary school students — is both precise and personal, a product both of the accumulated imagination of thinkers and doers from the past and of the individual learner herself.

Nonetheless, work of a high standard — in each case meeting some reasonable definition — must be presented by all students, and there must be an end to the lamentable intellectual sloppiness one sees in too many American high schools. There is wide and important agreement on that. The task is to achieve that end even when the definition of serious high-quality work is always itself in motion, and to achieve it in a climate of diversity and academic freedom.

Standards must be set for educators and politicians as well as for students. To hold students accountable for high-quality scholarship in a school system that is inadequately funded, roiling with political wars, and suffering from highly unstable leadership is not fair. Then too there are Horace's compromises. How must the routines of school be reformed if we are to achieve high standards for all children? Put negatively, can a high school be considered of high standard if it saddles each teacher with 135 students?

Behind all this is the question of who ultimately sets the standards. This is a matter of practical democracy, involving the legitimate rights of parents to have major authority for the schooling of their children. The state takes a long stride by insisting on the children's attendance at school. Can it justify a further stride by asserting virtually absolute control over the nature of the school attended, even if this is in the name of high standards (as they happen to define them)? Alternatively, if the people want choice and expect substantial control of their own children's schools, can the nation have high standards too?

The thicket of issues here goes to the heart of the place of compulsory education in a democracy, particularly in a democracy made up of diverse peoples and cultures. The United States has been helped by the flood of new ideas and curricula and assessments emerging from federal and philanthropic investment in standards-based reform. The issue of quality and the need to hold students (and their schools) accountable for significant work is clearly before the public. Also before the public are the complex implications of a quest for "world-class standards" — even though such standards do not and never could or should exist. The debate has barely started.[8]

Systemic reform

Americans have long had a great love affair with what they call "order." They have admired bureaucratic systems for the conduct of education. They have put their faith in elaborate mechanisms of control, with the folks at the top providing carrots and sticks to manage those at the bottom.

Such scientifically designed systems were the hallmarks of the American Progressive era. Of all such governmental arrangements, those governing public education have survived the longest. It is no surprise that in our time there has been use of the words "systemic reform." Another word sometimes used interchangeably is "restructuring," borrowed from business. The words may have changed, but the assumptions behind them go back to the first decade of this century.

Until the past few decades, however, "systemic reform" has referred to various efforts to reorder and streamline the educational hierarchy. The assumption all along was that the basic framework of the system — local districts, state authorities, and the federal government — would remain largely intact and the leaders of these domains, usually referred to (along with prominent business and civic leaders) as "stakeholders," would be at the table where the redesign was to be negotiated. The Clinton administration's Goals 2000 enterprise is representative of the process, being a piece of federal legislation that was in tune with what many governors wanted to mesh with their state efforts.

For a host of reasons, this process appears to have made little progress. The various stakeholders have hung on to their prerogatives. The case was never convincingly made that fixing the system would appreciably help the children. For people such as Horace Smith, the process largely missed the point. Few of the compromises that crippled his work were at all addressed by the various state plans. Finally, very little money was put behind the reform. Change was somehow to happen without any serious investment, except the application of threats.

My hunch is that money specifically and consistently targeted for reform activity was lacking not only because of straitened times. The lack was also likely due to misgivings on many leaders' parts. If the system that had been in place for almost a century did not work, and since some had earlier tried to fiddle with it, why fiddle again now? Why not start over again?

By the mid-1990s, the let's-start-over-again way of thinking could be recognized across the states, although it was rarely couched in such apocalyptic terms. Governors proposed sharp cutbacks and even elimination of state departments and state boards of education. Public support for private schools and vouchers, calling for a system financed entirely by state funds "given" to the family of each school-age child, with families choosing the school for that child, appeared and became serious topics of political conversation, albeit under different rhetoric and slogans, such as "public money should follow the child."

Systemic reform now stands for thinking of a new way to provide education, not merely fixing the system we have inherited. This is a break from almost a century of practice, with its dependence on a hierarchical bureaucracy. Given the inadequacies of the present system, the fresh conversation is a source of hope.

Multiculturalism

"Multiculturalism" has become a code word for America's biggest culture war. The battle is over what it is to be American, and the public schools, the principal public institution expected to purvey to the young the nature of that culture, are in the center of the fray.

The multicultural sentiment is an offspring of the civil rights movement of the 1960s, led by African Americans and subsequently joined by other racial and ethnic groups and by women. The general issues are simple and straightforward. Is the core of teaching in our schools to be in English? Is the social and literary heart of public school studies to be drawn from European and Judeo-Christian traditions, or are the schools to reflect the African, Asian, Native American, and Latino cultures of both a longstanding and growing part of the population with equal power? Passions are hot on all sides of this issue.

Since children of color or of non-European background represent a third or more of national public school enrollments, it is difficult to see, even in political terms, exactly how the cultural claims of their families can be denied.[9] The problem will be, then, to figure out how to meet these claims. Through a new cultural tradition, an amalgam of the different literatures, histories, and customs — in effect, a new conception of what being American signifies, embodied in a required school curriculum? Parallel curricula, each with a different cultural or linguistic focus, one for each group in a school — separate but equal, as it were? Radical choice among public schools — a Eurocentric school, an African American school, a Creole-speaking school, for example — with the parents deciding on which tradition will best serve their child? A knockdown, drag-out battle to retain the existing regimens?

The entire multicultural debate, which is unlikely to result in a conclusion satisfactory to all, poignantly reminds us of our constitutional tradition, which allows for ways to settle explosive issues of this sort. Without the Constitution, trust in it — even though it was a European and Enlightenment creation — and trust in its agents, this country could sink into a large-scale version of the splintered and genocidal Balkans.

The struggle for a new "one best America" — the best, perhaps, of the word "multiculturalism" — is with us, and it will affect the schools, however much many people want to sweep it under the rug. The matter cannot and should not be dodged, and reform plans that overlook it or impose simplistic, culturally insensitive remedies will certainly fail. Our condition can better be put positively: the strength of this country is in fact found in its spectrum of cultures. The trick now is to lessen our fear of each other and find and occupy our important common ground.

* * *

The slogans point a way, although yet dimly. Put in their best light, they suggest

- a school system that educates all children (not one that merely sorts the apparently apt from the presumably slow) to high standards (even though the definition of just what these are inevitably continues)
- schools that are sensitively accountable to several authorities (to families, not just the governmental hierarchy)
- a system that offers choice among schools (for everybody, not just those who can afford it; if necessary, across existing district lines) but at the same time insists on high standards for each school
- a school system that has some sort of national rationale (that makes sense not only for its particular students but for the larger society) but is also respectful of differences across the country
- a system with flexible administrative arrangements which function effectively within these emerging new imperatives
- schools that reflect the population as it is (rather than what some wish it was).

Language helps. Its suppleness provides a way for policy to take shape, sculptured from the effort at ever more precise and more persuasive definitions. Even slogans, pretentious though they at times may sound, can fuel serious reform. If Horace looks carefully, he can see an emerging star to give direction.

◆ New Schools in Suburbia

The senior was alone onstage, giving her senior project performance to an audience of parents and visitors. The topic was Martha Graham, the great American dancer. The student opened with an easy and informal but obviously well-prepared recitation about Graham's life and work. She then moved to a critique of the dancer's method, turning on a boombox and demonstrating for the audience. She performed and analyzed, performed and described. Questions from her audience followed. When her hour was up, she suddenly showed her tension and exhaustion, glistening in response to the reactions of the crowd. Her performance had been an engrossing mix of biography, dance theory, performance, and introspection, a piece of serious work that met a high standard. It was terribly important to her, more than just a requirement for school.

Many of her classmates at New Hampshire's Souhegan High School were elsewhere in the building on this late May evening, presenting their own final work. Much had already been subjected to judgment by the faculty during regular schooltime. This after-hours, voluntary occasion was designed to show the community (especially Mom and Dad) where much of the spring's work had gone, whether in the arts, in science, or in a project of active and reflective social service. The building hummed.

The gymnasium in Georgia's Salem High School, as grand in its way as Souhegan's theater, was now decked out for graduation, the first in the school's history. An enormous crowd was present. The graduates were smartly dressed and paraded around both solemnly and jubilantly. All who were graduating were involved, including a few youngsters with serious handicaps; while their diplomas were of a different kind from those of others, they were part of the class. Their peers warmly accepted them, helping them along as necessary.

The four student speakers had been selected by their classmates rather than by a computer calculating grade-point averages. There were a valedictorian and a salutatorian, both enthusiastically recognized, but the speakers had been selected for their demonstrated ability at such a task and because of their peers' respect for their views. Their performances were exemplary, worthy at moments of demanding college-level work. It gave a sheen to what is often a perfunctory end-of-year ceremony, tightly controlled by platoons of assistant principals. There was order at Salem High, but there was exuberant dignity as well. And there were demonstrations of high-quality work.

Across the country, most affluent communities are served by high schools that are generally perceived by their publics to work. They do so in some significant respects, most importantly by sending the large majority of their graduates on to higher education and a fair proportion to very selective universities. Most of their students know how to play the expected academic game. Their communities are free of blatant violence. Their families are rarely on the move; the ninth-graders are likely to make it to graduation in the same place. The schools' physical plants are well tended. Their faculties are usually stable, and thus veteran, and the student loads carried by these teachers are generally much lighter than those carried by those who serve less affluent children.

One visits these schools and finds happy kids and earnest teachers. I know them well. I have taught in several, all fine schools deserving a good reputation.

A nagging question for many of us close to these schools persists, however. Why are the graduates of these schools not even more intellectually powerful and aware than they appear to be, given the advantages they have received? Apart from the academic superstars (precocious and committed young scholars who seemingly soak up work and have the time and protection to do so, who are prodded along and encouraged by their families, and who make those of us who teach them look terrific), these schools' students, those whom some have called "the unspecial majority," are often regarded as competent but uninspired.[10] Might a random sampling of the essays of all of a school's eleventh-graders, not just the stars of the literary magazine, be impressive? How many have studied calculus or engaged at a high standard in some serious artistic pursuit? How many can carry on an interesting and well-informed conversation about current cultural and political matters with skeptical adults?

Many teachers in such schools clearly believe that not many high school seniors, even ones who have benefited from all sorts of advantages, would perform at all well. Concern about this has encouraged some teachers and administrators serving stable and relatively affluent communities to think freshly about their work. In some growing communities new high schools are being built, and in Conyers, Georgia, and Amherst, New Hampshire, the responsible school boards insisted on plans that reflected a more demanding and sensible regimen than the traditional one. Conyers's Salem High School and Amherst's Souhegan High School were designed from scratch as Essential schools, drawing not only from the Coalition's experience but also from various regional initiatives, such as Foxfire in Georgia. At the same time, both schools had to be careful to respond to local sentiment that some long-serving school practices seemed to work well enough. Given that opinion, some parents believed that any "experimenting" with their offspring had to have clear and readily defensible bounds.

Souhegan and Salem followed some similar paths. Both designed curricula that stressed both traditional disciplinary work and demanding interdisciplinary work. Both grouped students and teachers in teams. Both developed a curriculum of questions, forcing the students to engage intensely in their work. Both insisted on regular and public exhibitions of the students' work. Both — and this has been controversial — group their students heterogeneously. Salem calls this "teamstreaming": each student is in effect on a personal track within the team and is expected to aim high. Salem has an honors program, and Souhegan encourages its students to take Advanced Placement tests offered by the College Board and allows any student who so chooses to strive for an "Honors Challenge," an extra bit of demanding work; at both schools every student can join in and try.

In both schools this policy initially attracted flak. Parents who believed their children were gifted wanted them taught in classes with only gifted children. The two principals, and their superintendents and school boards, stood their ground on this issue. Every child was expected to achieve at a high level. No child was assigned to any permanent and self-fulfilling rank. Every child was pushed as hard as possible, the academically swift no less than any other.

The proof has been in the pudding. Souhegan's and Salem's seniors have met or exceeded traditional academic expectations, including those for college entrance as well as test scores. Other gains are subtler — reports from families that their children have done far better than they had dared to hope, the student who finds self-confidence, the sense of community that has developed among students throughout the school.

Salem experienced an anomaly with its first graduating class, which, although somewhat smaller than parallel classes at other high schools in the county, pulled in twice the usual amount of college scholarship dollars — over $2 million — from outside sources. Was this simply luck? Was it due to the persistence of Salem's college counselors? Or did Salem's seniors exhibit special poise and responsibility during the interviews for many of these awards — adult qualities derived from four years' experience with public Exhibitions at which they had to explain their ideas and field serious questions? While the truth probably lies with all three, the third is especially thought-provoking, particularly considering the scale of the achievement.

Personally, I picked up the spirit at both these schools through the sharpness and the courtesy of the questions about Essential school ideas I received from students when I visited. Like many high school students, these were deeply involved in their schools' lives, but at Souhegan and Salem the students were especially invested in the heart of the matter — the whats and whys of the teaching they received and of their own personal learning. They were conscious about how they learned and why, a quality that will serve them well in the future.

Salem High School, Conyers, Georgia; Robert Cresswell, principal. Member of the Coalition of Essential Schools since 1991. Salem is a Next Generation School for Georgia and a Georgia Demonstration School for High School Restructuring.

Souhegan High School, Amherst, New Hampshire; Robert Mackin, principal. Member of the Coalition of Essential Schools since 1992, Souhegan was New Hampshire School of Excellence in 1993–1994. Robert Mackin was 1995 New Hampshire Principal of the Year and a finalist for the NASSP National Principal of the Year award of 1996.

4

The Work of Reform

SOUHEGAN AND SALEM HIGH SCHOOLS were launched by communities that thought through in some detail what values they and
therefore their school should reflect. Both these schools were new. They
started with a corps of leaders who agreed on most fundamental matters. They had at the outset the star Horace is looking for to give
direction.

Developing such a star in an ongoing school is more difficult; redi-
recting a Tillson or even a Carney will take a more heroic effort. Each
has its old academic baronies, good and bad. The faculty has had battles
in the past, and these will have left unforgotten scars. The drag of
tradition and the weakness of incentives to do much that is different are
substantial.

However, difficult though it may be, defining a school's goals and
standards is easy work compared with putting them into practice. Most
of what many schools call "vision statements" are as excessively grand
as they are engaging, and getting them to function is often a morale-
wrenching activity. There will always be compromises, the need to
make painful choices among virtuous options. It requires stubbornly
persistent work to accomplish this, and keeping the faculty's collective
eye on what is more and what is less important.

Two schools that I recently visited, both participants in the Coalition of Essential Schools, reflect this phenomenon. The first is Massey High School, a commanding but now shabby three-story stone building sited on a large lot behind a strip of small stores, fast-food restaurants, and boarded-up homes. A scruffy field extends behind, providing not enough space for activity by many of the school's 750 pupils. A parking lot surrounded by a chainlink fence adjoins the large late-1930s school building. A solid steel door bedecked with graffiti confronted me when I attempted to enter. The security guard signed me in and directed me to the principal's office.

My visit was carefully orchestrated. First I had a chat with the senior administrators, all of us having coffee in mugs decorated with the school logo and motto: *Go Tigers!* The mood was sober, realistic, but still optimistic. A student then arrived to show me around. We made brief visits to a few classes, these room-by-room forays serving more to interrupt each lesson than to enlighten me, and ended with an extended session listening to the massed concert band practicing Brahms's Academic Festival Overture.

Luncheon with the faculty followed, in a small lounge off the cafeteria. Teachers came in and out; since their contract with the district had recently been amended to give them a "nonsupervisory lunch break," they got their twenty or forty minutes (depending on the vagaries of the complex teaching schedule) apart from the students. If they chose, they could spend it eating with their colleagues at small round tables in this oasis far from adolescents.

This school was trying to reshape its work, or as the jargon has it, to restructure. The faculty members had read about the Coalition of Essential Schools and were proceeding with a plan derived from ideas they had gleaned there. The administration had advised them that I would be in the lounge to chat with them and to answer questions.

The conversation was awkward. Most people concentrated first on their bag lunches (few turned to the school cafeteria for their meal). There was talk of the immediate — of a recent basketball game, of a parents' night which had had sparse attendance, of an altercation in the gym, of the push for recognition for a gay and lesbian student organization, of a rash of gang confrontations in the nearby city park.

Some came to my table; others went elsewhere in the room, avoiding conversation. Quickly I sensed that those with me were mostly teachers in the Essential school pilot program. I asked them how they were doing.

They spoke of the difficulties first, then the rewards. The kids did not like the pressure to do more on their own and to present their work publicly, such as (for a U.S. history class) making and defending a case in favor of the 1890 Sherman Anti-Trust Act. Standing up to questions from an audience of teachers and parents was tough for them. They alternately cursed and reveled in the attention the new regimen afforded them. They understood that they were on a new sort of academic hook, and they resented that.

Although the administration supported the new program, the details of school kept getting in the way. The bells rang at inappropriate times. The city computers that scheduled the students (by central office order) were incapable of handling the new Essential school pattern of classes. The second-level district administrative staff did not seem to understand how much freedom the Essential school teams had been promised. Glitches abounded, mostly dealing with the trivial but with untrivial consequences.

The likelihood of new budget cuts imposed on the district created a pervasive gloom. New state and district mandates kept adding things to cover, threatening to bloat the carefully slimmed-down program designed by the Essential school teams — quartets of teachers from mathematics, science, English, and social studies departments who had been assigned two-and-a-half-hour daily blocks of scheduled class time to work with a common group of 110 ninth-grade students. The state tests rewarded the display of straightforward memory work, not the use of knowledge. If the students were to be judged on the basis of such tests and not more sensible and demanding ones, in what sort of jeopardy did that place the new program?

I pondered the basically negative temper of the talk. Why complain to me? To show me how hard the work was? I already knew that, and they knew I knew it. To show me how little support from the top they got? If so, why not be wholly explicit about what had to be done about the matter? The most plausible explanation was frustration and the need to vent. I was a convenient (and, I gathered, rare) audience. Few folks came to listen to these teachers.

The litany of complaints continued. Even after a Herculean effort by the staff to reach out to families, parents still did not seem really to understand or appreciate what was going on. There were no subject-matter materials that supported the new kinds of teaching and learning. Teaching in teams was unfamiliar and stressful; each teacher was on show for the others. There was no money for relief, no planning time, no real help. Apparently the powers that be believed that reform was to happen merely by fiat — which meant that change was on the teachers' backs. It all was exhausting.

I began to feel dismayed. But then . . .

And exhilarating too, they said. The kids were coming alive. It was rewarding to know them better, something that was possible with the more focused academic program — a concerted and interconnected program in the four key subjects represented by the teachers. Team teaching helped too, they said; they all had the same kids and could discuss their work daily. The students' performance was better. They showed up. They depend on us, the teachers reported. They take our time, and while this stretches us, it is rewarding too. The kids engage more. It is nice to have colleagues, other teachers in the team on whom to lean from time to time. Some parents see a new energy for school in their children and tell us about it. We are going in the right direction.

All this was familiar. The better the teachers know the students, the more likely it is that the students will take, even demand, their time. Good teaching creates a bottomless hole of student expectations. The kids connect with a teacher and then want more of everything.[1]

The others in the lounge listened in, though they were trying not to show it. My tablemates did not remark on the stresses within the faculty, the jealousies among teachers that the start of restructuring had created. Everyone was polite. I heard of the faculty squabbles only later, from some of my luncheon partners who collared me privately in the hall.

My visit tapered off after the early afternoon classes and the rapid exodus of students to their jobs or, for a few, to athletics. Faculty members also left abruptly; there were two-job folks here. The shabby building was hushed by three o'clock.

The principal offered to take me to the airport, and I accepted. On the way she told me how frustrating it was to combine the endless crush of details of merely keeping school with the new demands of leading a reform effort. She directly criticized few of her school colleagues and district superiors, but she made it clear that she and her handful of eager teachers and parents had been left with paltry extra resources and at the same time a full load of "show me" expectations from the higher-ups. The status quo did not work, she lamented, but the full burden of proof still lay on the shoulders of those who tried to confront it by setting forth work for students that was demonstrably more sensible.

Once again I was an audience. I was reminded of how the job of school reform is a remarkably solitary one unless steps are systematically taken to build colleagueship. This is no surprise: teaching in most high schools is a solitary job — my kids, my classes, and my classroom, with a door to shut — and the principal often is no less isolated. Collective responsibility is honored in most schools only in the breach.

She railed a bit, but at the same time she asserted that she would pursue the reform or quit. She was upbeat as we pulled into the airport, seemingly refreshed by recounting her problems. Her passion when describing what her school might be able to do for kids gave me hope. But the description of the battle, with all its skirmishes and the absence of powerful friends who were stalwartly behind the effort, disheartened me.

The following day I visited a junior-senior high school in another city, a new, small establishment that was the dream of three veteran teachers who had been itching to try their hands at creating a school from scratch, one that squared with their view of what was effective with and for adolescents. Because student enrollments were growing in the city, the district's superintendent had arranged for the establishment of several new small schools. Better that, he argued, than creating a few vast schools that were ungovernable at worst and inefficient at best.

The program had only 110 students so far, 50 who were twelve and 60 who were thirteen. They were housed in an old elementary school building which had been in mothballs until recently. During the 1980s, enrollments had fallen. The new school, called the Contreras High School after a local hero, shared the space with an elementary school serving seriously handicapped pupils.

It was difficult to find the office, which turned out to be a classroom jammed with desks, copiers, folding tables with books and papers spilling across them, blackboards covered with messages for this or that person, coats and hats and boots piled into corners — a jumble of activity, half-organized chaos. The school secretary presided over all of this from a table in a corner, armed with one of the aged Macintosh computers ubiquitous in schools and a telephone.

I met with the faculty steering committee, which, despite its name, included two students and several parents. The discussion was about "student conduct." Apparently a wallet had been stolen, and while the usual process was for Contreras's Student-Faculty Fairness Council to deal with the matter, the steering committee members saw this as a symptom of a larger problem, that of trust and safety. The discussion was intense, full of as much disagreement as good humor.

These were proud people who liked one another. The contrast with Massey High was striking. Most of the Contreras people were younger and less experienced, but they had, in their small compass, a community full of the give-and-take that makes for honest collaboration. They needed it, I knew, given the volatile student body that they had attracted.

Of course, these feisty folk had gathered themselves to start a school. None had been assigned to this task: they had sought it. None had been "just there" in an existing school which, like Massey, was trying to redirect its work significantly with essentially the same staff that had proudly run the place in the old way and with little moral and financial support from the outside.

I spent several hours in one big classroom during the morning. Students worked mostly alone or in small groups on a problem in physics, one that required them to use simple algebra. There was unending chatter, which I initially found distracting but which the kids apparently did not. They were a generation used to background music, I thought. The two teachers (I discovered that one was in fact a student teacher from a local college) moved among them, checking work, cajoling here, explaining there. Periodically the class was called to order and one or another group was asked to present its findings, or at least the methods it was pursuing to arrive at findings. Some simple homemade physical apparatus was in a corner; various groups made their presentations at this contraption, explaining and demonstrating how they got their data.

How can anyone work in this apparent chaos? I wondered. The very easiness of the place might mean that everything was *too* easy. Little serious learning is wholly easy — exhilarating, often, but a necessary slog. One has to try hard to learn, and it is difficult to try if distractions abound. However, what might be distracting to me might easily be blotted out by a younger person.

I spent the afternoon in an arts class, again held in various modes over a two-hour span. There were some forty youngsters here, probably grouped for this exercise on the basis of their ease with reading and language. On the wall of the classroom was a permanent chart with bold letters listing "The Big Questions":

1. From whose viewpoint are we seeing or reading or hearing?
2. How do we know what we know? What is the evidence, and how reliable is it?
3. How are things, events, or people connected to each other? What is the cause and what the effect? How do they fit together?
4. So what? Why does it matter? What does it all mean? Who cares?

This reminded me of the list first compiled and used at New York City's Central Park East Secondary School.[2] Clearly Contreras's faculty had done some useful school visiting and constructive borrowing of ideas that appeared to be effective.

The large classroom — actually a double room, with the acoustical dividers pulled back — was a bustle of activity and steady noise during the entire afternoon. To me, standing back by a wall, it too appeared without order, albeit intensely purposeful. Here a group was poring over some texts. Further away another group was acting out some lines, obviously from a play. On this side two kids were talking intensely with a teacher; the adult was sharply challenging the kids and their work. Another adult was critiquing what appeared to be exercises in public speaking and movement.

These students, like the morning class, were called to some semblance of order so one of the teachers could clarify a point that appeared to him to be generally misunderstood, a matter that had crystallized from his eavesdropping on various groups. The youngsters barely tolerated this interruption, clearly waiting for the talk to be over so they could get back to their efforts, whatever these were.

It emerged that the matters of study were the concepts of evil and loyalty. The text was Shakespeare's *Othello*. The task for each student was first to read (carefully, repeatedly) a brief, relevant portion of the text and then, in association with his or her group, to prepare a segment of the play for performance as part of a classwide production of "Scenes from Shakespeare's *Othello*." Each group not only had to cast, stage, rehearse, and perform its segment; its members had to explain to the ultimate audience — other teachers dragooned into coming to the event and some parents, particularly, the teachers hoped, those who might have had some experience with the world of letters — their reasons for selecting their scene or scenes, what this segment meant to them, and why they staged it as they did. Out of this was to evolve a well-fashioned definition and description of the abstractions "evil" and "loyalty."

I noticed that there were five adults in the room. I learned later that two were regular teachers, one was a student teacher, and two were volunteers, both parents of kids at the school. One was a currently unemployed actress, and the other, as he put it, was "just a dad" who was taking the volunteer hours he had tithed away from his place of work.

As I watched this extraordinary scene, I conjured up comparable images. A Breughel painting of a marketplace. An architects' charrette. A congeries of bull sessions. An actors' master class. Christmas morning in the living room when all the kids first play with their new toys. A lecture. An inquisition, genial but demanding and confrontative nonetheless. All fit and none fit. The activity kept shifting, repacing itself.

What was common to it all was how intensely interested in the heart of this work most of the children were most of the time. Yes, there was goofing off and chitchatting and the horsing around that comes with brand-new hormones. But there was far less of that than one usually expects to see when kids are asked to do some work on their own. Although there was the appearance of disorder in the room, order of a sturdy kind almost surely was developing in the heads of those students. Or so the student teacher, quite pumped up and eager to impress me, whispered. I could not tell at the moment whether she was right or wrong. It was clear, however, that these were active students who were demonstrably engaged in puzzling out the meanings of good and evil.

This work in the arts, effectively on two themes in *Othello,* was to dominate a full week of these students' time. "Better that they learn well what one great text can give them than hop, skip, and jump around a bunch of texts," one of the teachers explained to me. I realized that one could not get a true sense of it all until one saw the students' final work.

I ended the day with the principal. She talked more of the troubles in her school than of things that she felt were going well. "It's so much harder to teach this way," she said, by which she meant in faculty teams and by pressing the students hard with questions so that by answering they would gain deep understanding of some important abstractions. "It is easy to control the material," she explained, "to dish it out, to tell the kids to kick it back . . . To provoke and challenge kids all the time — that wears you out. Burnout is a big worry."

This was more venting. The work is as hard as it is new. The kids were already at risk, and the teachers did not want to increase this risk; indeed, they wanted to help the children overcome it. The stress showed.

The principal had more to tell me: "Our kids come weakly prepared from their elementary schools. We deliberately started this school as a junior-senior high school to capture the kids as young as the district would let us. We make this an inviting and interesting place, and they like it, but to be inviting is not necessarily to be rigorous. If the kids don't think hard, using what they know well, they won't make it out there." She tossed her head toward the window overlooking the busy street outside. "It's hard. It's annoying always to have to defend what we are doing for being unlike regular school. Don't people know that regular school is a disaster for most kids like mine?"

Her worries paled in contrast to the happy joshing among the teachers as they gathered their belongings from the mess in the corners of the office. These folks carried the jauntiness of pioneers.

Massey and Contreras are typical of grass-roots reform. They represent the difficulties of breaking away from practices that are as familiar to veteran teachers as they may be ineffective. Familiarity takes precedence over reform, especially if there are few strong incentives to teach in new ways. The courage to continue arises from the visible engagement of students in both these schools, many of whom might never have shown up at all, much less worked hard in class, and the heady colleagueship of teachers embarked on a sought-after voyage.

Today in America we have two movements directed at the practical reform of schools, one starting at the top, the other at the bottom. There is important momentum behind the movements. Each has national footing. Each is enormously well intentioned. Each speaks its own language, considers its own priorities. Each needs the other, in one arrangement or another.

Top-down reformers deal with the sweeping realities — the labor market, foreign competition, assessment theory, changing the system. Reformers at the grass-roots level squeeze into a little corner of one school and wrestle with the tensions generated by a bunch of teachers, which for them are more telling than global economic confrontations with Sony and Mercedes Benz. Or, in a happier place in a big school district, they work with exhausted and delighted ferocity on the edges of the system.

A division of labor among these two reform efforts might be fine if there was congruence of purposes and accommodation to facts. This is usually not the case — not because it is impossible but because few have seriously tried to accomplish it.

Systemic reform, even if exquisitely designed, can founder on the unwillingness or incompetence of teachers. Top-down plans are easy to sabotage: teachers can close their doors and do what they want. Any sort of national reform — a raising of standards, as this is commonly put — will therefore require more than grudging cooperation from professional staffs and parents, one by one, teacher by teacher, parent by parent. The nature of schooling requires that. There is no quick surgical strike from on high that will work.[3] The people doing the job have to believe in it. The students doing the learning have to believe in it.

Those working at the top have been especially galled by the view of many school administrators that the current barrage of criticism is merely a "public relations problem." "If we could only get the newspapers to print what is good about the schools," these administrators say. Denial seems a frequent refuge. Top-down folks are understandably frustrated and impatient. Reform from on high comes glacially, if at all. Or so it appears to the policy and business community.

However, neither is quick movement to be had at the bottom. The experience of every regional or national reform group such as the Coalition of Essential Schools is that the work is slow, often controversial, and easy (once again) to sabotage. Without steady support from the top — and such has been rare for Coalition schools — it is difficult, if not impossible, to make progress.[4]

Irrespective of their good intentions, leaders at the top can stymie serious and sensible efforts at the bottom. For example, many states have mandated thoughtful standards and frameworks that are to guide the schools in their work. A very typical example of such a product is Oregon's "Learning Outcomes and Academic Standards" proposals, published in late 1994.[5] The fragment quoted below is a small part of a comprehensive statement of what each young Oregonian must display in order to receive a Certificate of Initial Mastery, which the student is to receive at roughly sixteen years of age and when finishing a typical tenth-grade year. It makes up one of five standards within a domain called "Communication."

WRITE

- Convey a clear, focused idea or message with relevant supporting details appropriate to the audience.
- Demonstrate competence in communicating in a broad range of modes (including persuasive, narrative, expository, imaginative, and descriptive), forms (including essays, poems, stories, journals, and letters), and styles (including informal, formal, practical, and technical).
- Demonstrate depth of independent thought.
- Demonstrate organization, sentence fluency, and command of writing conventions, including spelling, grammar, usage, punctuation, paragraphing, and capitalization.
- Use specific, precise words.

This is a sensible, laudable standard. It asks for a reasonable base of writing ability, something that every youngster needs to assure any sort of options within the job market. It opens doors for expression of all sorts. It is a standard with which people across a wide political spectrum can agree.

The standard applies to all children. Every student is expected to meet it, however long that takes. This is a universal standard, not one for an elite. Or so Oregon and its colleague states, in comparable lists, unanimously assert.

So how will it be met?

To answer, one has to go back to the beginning. How does one learn to write? By reading effective prose and poetry and reflecting carefully on its method. More important, by writing and rewriting and writing some more, with an editor close by, someone who promptly and regularly criticizes, cajoles, suggests, insists, promotes, and encourages. The editor — a teacher, in school parlance — is crucial.

How many budding writers can one editor/teacher take on effectively at once? Exemplary expository writing courses for college freshmen are a good place to look, even though one assumes that most freshmen can write better than the typical fourteen-year-old and are likely to be both more mature and more motivated. The loads typically run from thirty per term (at well-endowed private institutions) up to sixty or seventy (at many state and community colleges). A typical English teacher in a high school in the Pacific Northwest has one hundred or more. The load agreed on by contract for teachers in New York City is 175. Given recent budget crises, the actual load of English teachers in typical Los Angeles area schools is 192, whereas the load in a well-regarded Chicago suburban high school is 130.[6]

So what actually happens in typical high schools, in Oregon and elsewhere? The most interested and self-directed students capture some of the time of their teacher/editors. *The rest — the majority — rarely write serious and carefully edited prose or poetry at all.* The ways in which high schools are organized and resources are distributed make serious teaching virtually impossible even for devoted and experienced teachers like Horace Smith. The "world-class standard," so easily set, is utterly unattainable in schools as they are currently structured. The writing standard is not an exception.

Not surprisingly, therefore, some high school teachers read sweeping, comprehensive lists of goals and standards such as the Oregon ones and curse. In fact, most teachers probably ignore the standard-setting process altogether. It is so remote from reality that they believe it deserves no attention. Its leaders (including the token teachers on the various panels) and their pronouncements will pass, or so some veterans predict. Basically, these teachers believe — perhaps cynically, or defensively, or accurately — that the public and the politicians cannot seriously care about ordinary kids in school if they deliver mandates that are utterly unattainable under current conditions.

Personally, I admire Oregon's writing standards. They deserve to be adopted. Either more teachers and more time (and thus more money, an improbable scenario) or the elimination of other standards and school programs will be required in order to make this writing objective realistically achievable. The latter option can be readily described and designed (as I have done in *Horace's School*). Getting it under way, however, calls for tough choices and tougher politics.

To be sure, there are gestures from the top in the direction of serious school reform at the bottom, and these droplets are eagerly bid for: a $25,000 planning grant for a school of a thousand kids; the provision of a "distinguished educator" to counsel the staff in a school building at state expense; more "school site management." However, these projects are often seen by generous as well as embittered veterans as sops, utterly irrelevant to the scale and nature of effort involved and meant to distract the public at large from facing the fact that the secondary schools as currently structured simply do not and cannot meet the kinds of standards we should properly expect for all children.

In all, there is an epidemic of bitter cynicism and a sense of betrayal, especially among the ablest school people. It mirrors the derision with which many at the top regard educators, especially "educational bureaucrats" and teachers, whom they "honor" in a manner that painfully reveals their condescension.

Nonetheless, the two movements must ally or realign themselves in more imaginative and respectful ways than they have. In some quarters, this process is under way, and increasing numbers of people bridge the two worlds. Given the new pressures on public education, such alliances or new resolutions are necessary not merely to smooth out the ways of the old hierarchical order but to foster a realization that the very rules of the game are being changed. This does not mean that the same people, drawn from the top and the bottom and organized in the existing arrangement, can fruitfully sit down yet again and imaginatively carve up their responsibilities. Both sides are tired, frustrated, talked out. Some new impetus is needed.

A better system could, for example, grow out of the alliance of individual schools — the students, teachers, parents, and neighbors — that share specific educational objectives, with these schools collaboratively designing and shaping what they collectively need at their top. That is, the initiative would come from the ranks rather than from the high-level planners, and the resulting organization — no doubt very lean and unobtrusive — would reflect this.

Or state government could promote wholly new kinds of schools, ones that deliberately break the traditional mold and circumvent existing state regulations, certification requirements, and the local apparatus of school boards, unions, and collective bargaining agreements. Today these are usually referred to as charter schools, as they gain their public status through charters issued directly by the state.

Or groups of educators, organized in not-for-profit or for-profit organizations, could present themselves as contractors to take over and independently manage the existing public bureaucracies, including their schools.

All three of these patterns are now seen in American communities. In New York City, networks of very new schools extend across the local districts and boroughs, with special status in the city and the state. Over a dozen states have charter schools fully under way. Private contractors administer parts or all of public school systems in a number of communities, and the idea of full-fledged autonomous clusters of schools is widely accepted.[7]

One way or another, what is top and what is bottom are being reinvented. We are seeing fresh designs for how a very local enterprise — a particular school serving particular families as well as the larger community — can function as part of a sympathetic and effective democratic system.

◆ *A System of Schools*

Evidence: How do we know what we know? *Viewpoint:* Whose ideas are these, and how and why are they presented this way? *Connections:* What does this relate to, what patterns does it form? *Suppositions:* What if something else figured here? *Relevance:* So what?

These five habits of mind make up the now well-known touchstone of one of the earliest and perhaps the best known of the Essential schools, Central Park East Secondary School, in East Harlem, New York City. This public school opened in the fall of 1985 as a small school of choice within the city. Its 450 students are enrolled without an entrance examination or any precondition other than the students' and families' interest; they are largely African American and Latino and come primarily from lower-income homes.

The curriculum at CPESS is sharply focused. Everyone studies humanities and mathematics/science (and little else) at the same standard until the Senior Institute, which students enter on the basis of exhibited mastery, usually around age sixteen. A student graduates from the Senior Institute, and thereby from the school, by meeting qualifications in fourteen areas, reflecting both familiar categories (for example, literature, science/technology, language other than English) and ones less frequently seen (autobiography, ethics, and social issues). All fourteen areas require a portfolio (for example, a folder containing a selection of work that the student and his teacher agree reflects his best effort). The student "defends" seven of these areas at an Exhibition before a committee of teachers and outsiders.

The record of CPESS since its opening day has been remarkable. Fewer than 5 percent of the students transfer out each year. Fewer than 3 percent drop out. Over 90 percent graduate, at age eighteen or a bit later, as they complete their Exhibitions. Over 90 percent of those who graduate are admitted to college, the majority to four-year colleges. Of those who have matriculated at college, over 90 percent are still enrolled or have graduated.

A description of the school's regimen, however, highlights the less visible part of its success. The school derives its demonstrably effective focus from *ideas* — these five habits of mind, which are relentlessly stressed — and from a deeply moving commitment to children and to democracy. It is, then, not so much CPESS's design that counts as the convictions of those who shape that design to the best interests of their particular students at a particular time.

The school's adults form a community of colleagues rather than an aggregation of credentialed professionals. Instead of each practicing his or her specialty according to a prearranged plan and being assigned to the school on the basis of some system over which the school has no control, they make up a serious (and joyful) community with the students' families — a community that is honest with itself, that governs itself democratically, and that is thus full of debate and passion. To the marrow of its collective bones it shares a commitment to these children, whose futures, so daunting in many ways, must be resolutely fostered.

CPESS was largely the creation of a group of teachers gathered by Deborah Meier, a kindergarten teacher and elementary school principal who had earlier started three small elementary schools of choice in East Harlem. Her record and that of her remarkable colleagues at these schools and at CPESS has been well chronicled recently, both in print and on film. Their story, in so many ways contrary to the conventional wisdom about school reform, is of enormous importance. It changes the very way in which "reform" is defined, from a systemic technological enterprise to one that is rooted in ideas about the human mind and in trust that a democracy dependent on small groups of people will shape and use these ideas toward worthy ends.

The approach is contagious, although it frightens those in government, the universities, and business who have little trust in anything beyond the supervisory bric-a-brac of administrative hierarchies. By the end of the 1980s the contagion had extended in important ways to a succession of New York City public school chancellors, to the leadership of a key union, and to the State Board of Regents and its commissioner. What has evolved over almost a decade — never easily, never by carefully prearranged plan, always seemingly by means of a string of immediate tactical decisions born of some immediate crisis and nurtured at critical moments by private foundations — is a cluster of like-minded schools led by people committed to collaboration.

Some organizational protection emerged for the high schools within the "alternative high school" superintendency created in the mid-1980s, which united a wide range of offbeat schools across all five boroughs. As schools like CPESS sought to have more influence and impact throughout the city and interest in copying their ideas grew, Meier and her friends launched the Center for Collaborative Education. A privately funded network of schools with a small paid staff, CCE took on the burden of dealing with visitors and the media and lobbying for change. More important, CCE served as a continuing seminar for the people involved in the growing number of small public schools, making it possible for them to share their ideas about learning and teaching better. Once the Coalition of Essential Schools was launched nationally, CCE signed on as its New York City affiliate.

As Essential schools grew in number in the state of New York, they were clustered in a "New York Region," whose offices were temporarily sited at CCE. When the Board of Regents launched its "Compact for Excellence" program in 1991, Commissioner Thomas Sobol turned to this group of urban, suburban, and rural schools to take the lead, asking that these Essential schools apply for state waivers and support as a group rather than as individual institutions.

During the early 1990s, as New York City's public school enrollments continued to grow, several new projects were initiated to support radical changes in the way secondary schools in particular were conceived. These included the Fund for NYC Public Education's New Visions project, which brought together middle and secondary school people as well as other community agencies to create "break-the-mold" designs for schools, some of which became Coalition schools. In addition, CCE and the Board of Education embarked on an ambitious redesign of two of the least successful of the city's huge high schools, called the Coalition Campus Project. Beginning in the fall of 1993, CCE helped initiate ten new high schools to replace the two failing old schools. Teachers and principals from older Coalition schools were recruited to help staff the new schools. Four CPESS teachers, for example, moved on to become directors and principals of the new schools, and old and new schools developed partnerships in support of change. By the fall of 1994, more than forty schools in New York were full members of CCE and the Coalition — bearing witness to the proposition that CPESS was not a special case and could in fact be respectfully replicated.

When Ambassador Walter Annenberg provided the financial opportunity to spur school reform "at the grass-roots level, where the students, teachers, and parents are," the Coalition Campus Project and CCE joined with three of the city's reform organizations to create a bold new project called the New York Networks for School Renewal. Supported by all the major players in New York City schools — the teachers' union, the Board of Education, the state commissioner of education, and the mayor's office — it proposed to rethink from top to bottom the way public education is governed. The design imagined several dozen networks of small schools serving a total of 50,000 students and functioning as the basic operating units of a new kind of system. Each network, composed of schools that voluntarily joined together, would develop its own governing, administrative, and accountability structures, would be relieved of many existing rules and regulations, and would be provided with more direct access to its funds — in effect, it would behave in important ways as a replacement for the traditional school district — a new kind of chartered district. The difference from conventional governance was crucial, however, to the network plan.

First, these networks are federations of individual schools, gathered because of shared educational convictions rather than geography. Each network is of "human-scale" numbers. To avoid command-and-control habits, the key school figures have to trust one another, and that implies that the company of leaders comprises fewer than two dozen people.

Second, all are schools small enough so that both teachers and families can know each other well, and all are schools of choice. Both families and faculties choose the schools, knowing well what these schools stand for and what is expected of them.

Third, what these schools decide to do in concert is the result of their collective decision; that is, the initiative is in the hands of those at the bottom rather than people at the top. The top is the servant of those below; governance of the network follows the schools' collective wisdom rather than that of people some distance away who hand down decisions for execution.

Finally, each network is itself a collective accountability system. Each network expects the state and other authorities to review, critique, and ultimately accept its system of accountability rather than require the schools to fit a mold created far from the relevant communities. For purposes of accountability, these networks depend both on the market (the schools have to recruit and hold a student body) and on substantial — indeed, unprecedented — public exposure on a regular basis of their own and their students' work.

All four of these characteristics suggest new ways of looking at the public governance of the people's schools. They represent an important philosophical shift, giving much more authority and responsibility to school communities than to the administrative systems of which they are a part. In so doing, they redefine the locus for the democracy of public education. Only time will tell if the key players in New York will stay the course or slip back into earlier administrative habits, however discredited.

Much recent school reform, including that undertaken by the Coalition of Essential Schools, has been on a school-by-school basis. With painful accuracy, our approach has been derided as Hercules trying to cleanse the Augean stables with an ice cream scoop.[8] Clearly, there has to be a reform system, something beyond isolated, individual schools.

In response, the leaders at CPESS and their many friends in New

York have approached the creation of such a system resolutely from the angle of where the reform must originate — from the individual schools themselves. They envision a creative and persuasive combination of these schools which becomes a system. Such an approach is significantly different from the familiar approach of evolving a system by means of a large-scale and detailed master plan, which ultimately allows only certain kinds of controlled implementation at the grass-roots level.

Central Park East Secondary School is a place driven by explicit convictions about learning, convictions embodied by all in the school with utmost seriousness. Successful schools such as CPESS reveal the extension of that approach to the appropriate democratic governance of education, where authority rests disproportionately with those where the educational buck always stops — teachers and families of students.

In 1993, CPESS received an Innovations in State and Local Government Award from the Ford Foundation and the John F. Kennedy School of Government at Harvard University.[9] Deborah Meier is now a senior fellow at the Annenberg Institute for School Reform at Brown University.

Central Park East Secondary School, New York, New York; Paul Schwarz and David Smith, codirectors. Center for Collaborative Education; Heather Lewis and Priscilla Ellington, codirectors. The New York Networks for School Renewal; Douglas White, director, Deborah Meier and Roscoe Brown, cochairs of Consultative Council. Division of Alternative Schools, New York City Board of Education; Stephen Phillips, superintendent.

5

What Matters

THE PROOF of school reform is to be found in the students. All ultimately turns on them and what kind of people they are after they graduate.

The stability of the schools that produce these people is a related concern. An effective school that is like a meteor, glittering one moment and gone the next, represents not reform but merely a happy episode for one particular batch of fortunate children. Successful reform delivers strong and persisting schools.

If one judges the worth of a school by the character of its students, the specific definition of that character is critical. What is an effective school for one person is not necessarily so for another. And while many can agree on specific goals for basic educational levels — for example, can the child read or not? — the rub comes when more complex matters are expected, and a serious secondary education must be about complex, and thus often controversial, things.

What I personally care about is fostering thoughtful and decent young adults, people who have an informed imagination and the restraint to use it wisely. I want them to be respectful skeptics, accustomed to asking "Why?" and being satisfied only with an answer that has as solid a base of evidence as possible. I care about how they use their minds, and all that they have learned, when no one is looking — that is, beyond any formal testing situation, in which they know that they are on the line. I care about their *habits* of mind.[1]

Traditionally, students have been measured against standards that expect them to know some important things and be able to apply that knowledge. In Horace's English class, for example, students must know what satire is. They must be able to define it. They must know the work of some classic satirists. They must be able to use this knowledge — to identify a satirical form in a new piece of literature and be able to defend their judgment. Further, Horace asks them to write bits of satire, so they experience the task of using the form and thereby understand its constraints.

Conventionally, this is as far as a high school goes, and it is as far as most tests in English go. As a result, satire is something that largely lives in the world of school English and not elsewhere.

I would go further. The student should be able to see and use satire in settings other than English class. The ridicule in a Thomas Nast or Herblock cartoon. The sneer in a political speech. The gestures, even the subtle ones, of an older brother or a boss on the job. The text of a clever piece of rap. The lampooning of a musical form. Even the antics of a marching band at a football game's halftime. In other words, the student should understand satire so well — as ridicule, irony, sarcasm, either hurtful or mirthful — that she can see it in many forms and know what meanings might be established in each instance. Young people should be able to use it and understand the effects of its use on others. Satire can make people cry or laugh or see deeply or all of these at once. It is a powerful human weapon and tool. To understand it means to be able to perceive it usefully in whatever expected or unexpected place that it emerges — and not just in Horace's English class on a test about the writings of Jonathan Swift, important though this may be. Swift's *A Tale of a Tub* is one entree to an understanding of satire, never an end in itself.

Finally, I want each young person to be in the habit of "knowing satire," almost instinctively sensing whether this device is being used and if so, to what effect. I want that young person, in whatever setting, to *know* the differences between satire and strictly factual exposition and to be ready to respond wisely to each. Such a person is one whom, in this respect at least, we call an educated human being.

Such a habit represents for me what high standards are. These are standards that I myself hold for Essential schools. They profoundly affect the way that good schools work. Schools satisfied with a lower standard — knowing something and being able to use it in familiar situations, without going further — can be less subtle and insistent places.

I believe that the educated person is as a matter of habit respectfully skeptical. In many school quarters, however, skepticism has a bad name. For too many, it connotes a lack of trust, superciliousness, and rudeness. The facts are the facts, it is assumed. However, all human advancement has depended on people's saying "Why?" and "What if?" Progress comes from seeing something new and compelling in the apparently familiar, teasing out fresh and often better conclusions on the basis of fresh and diligently sought-after evidence.

Good schools promote the habit of respectful skepticism — respectful in that it rests on evidence and carefully established argument but is ever asking questions such as "Just why might this be so?" and "Is there another way of explaining this situation?" All humans revel in this process of inquiry to some extent. Asking questions captures our minds more readily than memorizing somebody else's answers to yet somebody else's questions. Good schools surely push forward the best of what disciplined minds in the past have sent down to us, but always by displaying yesterday's conclusions fundamentally as questions that always need fresh answers.

I expect that many — but surely not all — Americans would agree with these goals, if anyone took the time to describe them fully. Students' work toward such goals will be damnably difficult to define universally and thus to market and assess. The ultimate evaluation of an Essential school — or any good school — will necessarily thus remain somewhat elusive, quite subjective, less crisply analytic than many might like. But the fact remains that however difficult it may be to identify and rate them by means of testing instruments, informed and imaginative and sensitively restrained people are what make for a good workforce, good families, and a good community.

I have learned that people fully understand these goals when they think of their own children, their own precious flesh and blood. They understand almost as well when they are given specific examples. Everyone knows such a person when he or she sees one, and no two are ever exactly quite alike.

But when we describe these goals, we hear the critics scoff. Can the child read? Can he write? Can he cipher? Can he do his percents? Does he know where Seattle and Singapore are? Has he read *Hamlet?* Of course such "basics" are important and should be respected. They can be measured and should be measured. But the standard for secondary schools should go far beyond them.

What we have found — to our continuing dismay, if not surprise — is that change in schools, ultimately raising their standards, is exceedingly difficult, and the incentives to undertake such change in most communities are very weak. The work is hard and teachers sometimes burn out. But we have also found much that is encouraging. Essential schools that have more or less "broken through" with their plans appear to help young people attain notably higher academic levels than were previously forecast for them, as conventionally measured. In such schools, attendance of both students and teachers rises, disciplinary problems decrease, more students graduate, college matriculation increases, and those who enter college make it through. Finally, we sense higher morale among teachers and students.

So although we are sobered by how hard it is to accomplish change, we are encouraged by the qualities emerging in the students at those Essential schools that have successfully done so. We recognize that the evidence to date is limited and fragmentary. But the trends, however preliminary, are absolutely in the right direction. Only time will tell whether these trends will turn into a sustained movement.[2]

We do know now that the status quo of shopping-mall high schools and lecture-drill-and-test systems demonstrably do not work for too many pupils, and that the skimpy tests that are often administered distort and mask the depth and shape of our problems and seriously mislead the public. Maintaining this system while waiting for some foolproof new model is utterly irresponsible. We should act now on what we know. It is clear that tackling change is less risky than stubbornly sticking to old and discredited habits.

What have we in the Coalition of Essential Schools learned after a decade's experience? The question cannot easily be answered, as Essential schools do not begin by implementing a specific model with readily identifiable characteristics. Rather, Essential schools craft their own local model of a better school in response to a set of *ideas* commonly accepted within the Coalition (now dubbed the nine common principles; they appear in Appendix A). What we have learned arises from watching and appreciating the complex efforts of schools that are shaping a design appropriate to their own situation and true to these ideas and that are putting that design into effect.

A baker's dozen of observations — in effect, findings — deserve mention.

1. *The leap from traditional school practice to commonsense reform is for most Americans a heroic one.* Contrast familiar life outside school with that commonly found inside school. Few parents want to spend, or can even rationally contemplate spending, a full day all alone penned up in one room with twenty-seven twelve-year-olds, day after day. Indeed, the idea would reduce them to incredulous laughter. Most parents shrink at the prospect of running a two-hour-long birthday party for a dozen twelve-year-olds. Most parents would be especially concerned if they did not know some of these partying preteens or if some of the children came from a different part of town or spoke only a strange language. Most parents would gag at the prospect of asking those kids to do some serious sustained work rather than just have fun. Most parents would be indignant if someone else told them exactly how this birthday party was to be run. Nonetheless, most parents assume that a middle-school teacher can cope well every day of the week with five groups of twenty-seven twelve-year-olds drawn from every sort of community, following a regimen over which that teacher has almost no control.

Most college English department faculty members would mightily object — and do strenuously object — if those of them who teach writing classes are forced to carry more than sixty students at once, in four classes of fifteen students each. Nonetheless, most school boards assume that high school English instructors can teach 120 to 180 students, in groups of 20 to 40, to write clearly and well.

Few businesses hire people on the basis of test scores alone, or even principally so. Most businesses hire people on the basis of evidence about their previous work, its substance and how faithfully and imaginatively they dealt with that substance. Yet most policymakers assume that for serious purposes of judgment one can pinpoint the present effectiveness and future chances of a child, or even an entire school, on the basis of some congeries of numerical data.

Few successful businesses change the content of each employee's work every hour and regularly and insistently interrupt the workers' efforts with announcements on a public address system. Nonetheless, a seven- or eight-period day and an incessant blare of administrative matters over PA systems characterize most high schools.

Few serious enterprises let all their employees take long vacations at the same time every year. Few such enterprises assume that all work can be reduced to a predictable schedule, which implies that every worker will produce at the same speed. Few serious businesses believe that those who are immediately swifter are always better. Nonetheless, most high schools accept these practices without challenge.

And more. The typical routines of high school — the ones that force Horace into unhappy compromises — often defy elementary logic and the experience of the typical citizen. Yet, curiously, they seem exceedingly difficult to change.

I believe that there are at least four reasons for this extraordinary gap between common sense and common school practice.

First, high schools in America serve more symbolic than substantive purposes. The routines of adolescence carry great weight — taking the expected courses, coping with Mom and Dad over a report card festooned with challenging letter or numerical grades, meeting girls or boys, dating (made possible by the rituals of the high school hallways), attending homecoming, the prom, and above all graduation, that choreographed rite of passage expected of every American around the age of eighteen. One messes with these very familiar icons of practice at one's peril. So what if Horace has to compromise with some of his kids? Who really cares, especially if it means changing the familiar and comforting routines, routines the children have their hearts set on?

Second, the high school mechanism is highly complex and interconnected. The curriculum, for example, is divided into familiar subjects. To teach a particular subject in a public school, one has to be formally certified in that academic area by the state. One gains certification by attending a college where specified courses leading to that credential are given. The college is divided into departments that correspond with the certification needs of those at the high school. College faculty get their tenure by providing the expected courses and writing their books in the expected areas. The collective bargaining agreements reflect these subject categories. State and federal assessments and regulations depend on them. As a result, for Horace's Franklin High School to shift its academic organization from the utterly separate subject-matter categories of English, art, music, foreign languages, and theater to a collective and team-taught domain of "the arts," every one of these estates must be challenged, and, not surprisingly, many will resist the proposed changes. Seemingly everything important within and outside a high school affects everything else. To change anything means changing everything. The prospect is daunting, usually paralyzing.

Third, and not surprisingly, school routines tend to be remarkably similar in high schools across the country, even those in the private sector, where one might expect significantly different approaches. There are few examples, especially state-endorsed examples, of schools organized in ways and on assumptions that diverge sharply from the conventional. Thus we have a chicken-and-egg problem: there is no critical mass of different schools across the country to bear witness to a better kind of schooling, and this makes the argument in their favor a difficult one, based on promises rather than evidence.

Finally, the people who make many crucial decisions about educational policy and practice — those at the top — do not have to live with those decisions. After giving the order to charge, they do not have to lead the troops — that is, to serve directly in the schools. Accordingly, there is little incentive for many of them to study the realities of Horace's world carefully. They can require and recommend and finance with little immediate accountability. If kids do not improve, someone else is always there to blame. Dealing forthrightly with Horace's compromises would upset many parts of the establishment, and so the better part of valor is usually to add only where there will be little opposition. It is easier, for example, to insist on more in-service teacher training and to add new tests than to address the issue of student loads per teacher. It is easier to accept the traditional curriculum framework, one taught in a procession of periods, than to ask for the shaping of a significantly more sensible academic regimen. If maintaining a dysfunctional status quo causes little personal threat, why tackle that status quo in ways that are likely to cause pain?

Change comes hard, even when the need for the change is blatantly obvious. The system carries on, even when the carrying on is irrational. In Essential schools as well as in schools in kindred projects, there is usually a battle over even the most obviously needed reforms. Realistically, we must expect that a majority of the schools attempting significant change will flounder, smothered by the forces of mindless tradition, fear, and obstruction, which, because of the complexity of high school work, are so easy to rally. As a result, we have learned to be very straight with the schools and with the authorities directing them about the rigors and costs of serious change.

2. *Focus and Exhibitions are important.* Essential schools ask their students to *exhibit* their work and to earn their high school diploma by means of demanding public Exhibitions. Exhibitions consist of the presentation and discussion of the students' actual efforts — their essays, arguments, and experiments. The schools ask for performances of each accomplishment rather than tokens of these efforts, such as standardized tests taken in isolation and without the challenge of follow-up questions.

All sorts of provocations can work well as Exhibitions, from Socrates' questions in his ancient garden to some of the better brain-teasers found in puzzle books. Each probes the depth of a student's understanding of ideas, and each should test that student's ability to express herself. Most require dialogue. One rarely plumbs a student's understanding well without probing for clarification and affirmation.

A complex example appropriate to a senior high school humanities course might be "What is slavery, and why might a caged bird sing?" The word "slavery" had a familiar and savage meaning in nineteenth-century America. It is also used today in a variety of contexts: *He is enslaved by drugs. I am a slave to chocolate. I am a slave to love. Mandatory attendance laws enslave American schoolchildren. I am a slave to familiar routines. I am your slave.* The student could be asked to describe different meanings appropriate to different times. She could be asked to portray in words or images the sense of enslavement, both vicious and benign. She might put together a portfolio of images of slavery from the different perspectives of others — the slaves and the enslavers — in the past. In rendering differing definitions and depictions, the student and her examiners could get a fair sense of her understanding of the highly complex idea of enslavement, the consequences of that idea as its various definitions play out, and her ability to express these abstractions persuasively. And they could get a sense of whether she has grasped the deep subtleties of language — the word "slavery" being a powerful example — and connected these with images and human experience.

With Exhibitions, the students must expect to be challenged. They have to be able to display their knowledge and explain it. They have to understand the material well enough to respond to questions that probe that understanding. The record of their exhibited work over time — some call these portfolios — can signal the extent to which their understanding is deep and to which they use it as a matter of habit.[3]

The idea of Exhibitions derives as much from common sense as from custom. We do not judge a high school's marching band and the individual players within it on the basis of brief snippets of taped music and videos of the marching. We want to see and hear that marching band in a real place, under real conditions, performing its entire repertoire, over time. The band ultimately knows full well how it is regarded, and why. At the same time, if well led, its members have a sense of what the target is, of how competence and excellence in this sort of endeavor is defined. They know from the observation of other, more experienced bands what they are aiming at, and they know that they have to go public and display their individual and collective work. This is a powerful incentive.

The Essential schools have learned that the idea of Exhibitions can and must be applied to all schoolwork. It forces everyone to focus on what the target is. What matters is the work of the students, not the means to that end, whether cooperative learning, "whole language" work, or the diagramming of sentences. The proof of all those and other worthy puddings must be found in the students' performance.

Courses cannot be described merely as "covering the twentieth century" or "reading works by Twain, Hemingway, and Updike." Teachers and students have to work out how a topic can be deployed intellectually to go beyond the immediate facts covered in class and be displayed in some form for interested observers. The products of study have to be clearly exhibitable; they cannot just be described by what the teacher or the student does during the process of learning. The meat of it is the expression and the use of the learning itself, at a standard that people can see and hear.[4]

What is expected should be clear, and the school must be able to justify it readily to students and their parents as worthy of serious effort on its own terms, not just as something to do well at to "get a good grade" and then to discard.

The effect of Exhibitions on Essential schools and the focus they provide have been substantial.[5] They have provided criteria for setting priorities. They have forced faculties to be clear about what the students have to do and why. Drafting them has illuminated the overlaps and interconnections between subjects and made it possible for teachers to use an interdisciplinary approach whenever it seems to benefit their students.

Exhibitions have forced faculties to relate these expectations to their particular students. Given where *our* students are, a faculty must say, what do we start with, what do we stick to, what must be done above all other things? Typical high school faculties rarely talk collectively of these matters. The Exhibitions provide a powerful impetus to do so. The point is made by the reverse, by faculties that do not grapple with the issue of specific, persuasive intellectual targets for their students and thus make little headway in improving student work. By forfeiting the powerful incentives that Exhibitions provide, their students suffer.

We have learned that nothing is more difficult for Essential school people than this work with Exhibitions. It demands thinking about learning and the curriculum and teaching and assessment differently from the ways in which most of us were trained. It forces us as never before to ask, "What is good enough?" — a question that was previously kept private between students and each of their teachers.

Going public brings sloppy work to light. It can also lead educators to discover that many students who have been labeled "superior" or "incompetent" in fact are at neither extreme. We have learned how distressingly weak many students — perhaps most students — are, even in the advanced sections at high schools. They may be able to tell us things, but too often they are not able to explain why those things are so or to use what they have learned in a new context. The clarity of the Exhibition process is both illuminating and sobering.

During their first years, Essential schools that use public Exhibitions often are at once interesting and turbulent places. For many teachers, students, and parents, Exhibitions mark a new way of expressing expectations for students, the process of learning, and the actual substance of an education. It is demanding work. However, those Essential schools that have been using Exhibitions long enough to see the effects clearly strongly attest to their importance. Exhibitions concentrate a school's priorities in the right place.

3. *If students are to understand deeply, less is more.* An oft-stated goal, found in virtually every state framework for student achievement, is "the ability to think critically and creatively and form reasoned judgments."[6] Now take a topic that should be a staple of any high school social studies curriculum: immigration to the United States. What does it take to "form reasoned judgments" about this explosive issue, both historically (for example, we extol ourselves as a "nation of immigrants") and in terms of contemporary politics?

A student would have to know something of consequence about a variety of matters. Geography (who lives where and under what circumstances). American demography, present and past. Global demography, present and past. American "customary convictions" over time (the way we have greeted or excluded "outsiders" during our history, our reasons for these policies, and how we think and feel about them today). Immigration law. The economics of the American labor force, past and present. The ecology of areas being abruptly and heavily settled. The costs and practical realities of immigration to the immigrant (in 1900, there were no Boeing 747s to whisk large numbers of people quickly across oceans at remarkably low cost). Human justice and the justice of the legal system. The biases of the political establishment (in part, a moral dimension). And more.

To rush through the topic of American immigration in a day or two — the usual recipe — guarantees superficiality and reinforces the habit of dealing with important matters hastily and thereby largely with slogans, many of which have been casually picked up from the media, from a textbook, from particular teachers, or from family members. To get the rudiments of a serious understanding of this issue requires both time and the investigation of a number of currently unconnected subjects in the high school curriculum (for example, history, economics, statistics, ecology, geography).

The function of secondary education is not so much to get students to understand the immigration question as to get them to understand how an issue such as immigration can be understood. That is, the substance of the matter is but an important foil for enduring intellectual habits. Sloppy work will lead to sloppy habits.

Of course, even after giving major attention to the immigration issue, high school students will not become experts in this field. What they will gain, however, is a sense of the wide sweep of important influences on an issue of this sort and humility about what they now can and cannot say about the matter. From such humility — an awareness of the complexity of things and of all that one does not yet know — comes deep understanding.

None of the nine common Essential school principles has caused more problems than this one, which calls for doing carefully limited, crucially important things exceedingly well. Tradition calls for sweeping coverage of topics. Existing curriculum guides and the achievement tests that accompany them reinforce this expanse of knowledge. Text-books so complete that they can hardly be lifted add to the message that coverage is king. Serious mastery is the victim. Only schools that have both the courage to go deep and support in that practice from their school districts have been able to succeed.

Such, then, is "less." Where, many ask, is the "more"? The answer lies in the habit of serious learning. The student who knows how to get deeply into a topic, who has seen its complexity, and who has been held accountable for it in a demanding Exhibition knows the nature of high-quality work and is therefore able to demand it of himself in later life. However, a student who is in the habit of learning superficially, quickly forgetting most of the facts whisked by him, ultimately acts accordingly. That is, he has bad habits of learning and does not learn well. There is surely no sadder "less" than this for a high school graduate. He has had no significant practice in honing the ability to think critically and creatively and form reasoned judgments.

4. *The students have to do the work. We learn when we engage, the more intensely the better.* As the familiar slogan correctly has it, one has to think hard. One has to work at new ideas, new skills, new relationships. One learns little if one's mind keeps wandering. One rarely gets it — say, the functioning of a right triangle — without using it, or having to explain it, or applying it to a new situation.

Means follow ends. If the ends are cast in the form of student Exhibitions that require the kind of active defense that indicates thorough understanding, then the students' preparation for those Exhibitions must involve closely engaged work and experience in answering questions about what they know and why they know it. If an Exhibition requires a student not just to present a finding or idea but also to use it in understanding or solving an unfamiliar problem, then preparation must include the tackling of unfamiliar problems.

In contrast, if the ends are reflected in tests that require little more than recall, a student's simple memory work will suffice. She can dream in class, cram the night before the test, ace it the next day, and forget everything about it within a week. If no one ever asks the reason for an answer, then the student has no incentive to know why she is concluding a matter in a particular way.

If a writing test involves merely an essay composed quickly from scratch on the spot, then the student has little reason to work hard in school at drafts and redrafts. If the student is never asked any questions that require thoughtful use of ideas (for example, applying the geometry of the right triangle to the solution of a building problem), then he needs no experience in such exercises. If the ends are cast in the form of analogic questions or mental brain teasers that have nothing to do with the curriculum, then working hard at that curriculum makes little sense.

People work hard if there is an incentive to do so. Worthy ends — performances that the students admire or are persuaded to admire — provide an incentive. If those ends absolutely require intellectual engagement by the students, that engagement will follow.

Having high and clearly worthy expectations for young people gives them dignity. As we all remember from our own adolescence, dignity or something like it is a treasure. When we are taken seriously, when people assume that we can and will do things, the expectation becomes an elixir.

Unchallenged kids get the message. If adults expect little of them, expect that they must be reminded, hectored, hassled, expect them to be goof-offs, then they will goof off. Of course, some people will goof off no matter what expectations are set. But teachers should assume the highest standard of performance until they are shown that it is not forthcoming. This is the proper start for each young person's education. If that standard is substantial and persuasive — if it symbolizes the dignity of a demanding expectation — more often than not, adolescents rise to the occasion.

Essential schools have found that if the Exhibitions require an active defense and a demonstration of the use of knowledge, then the practice for such work has to include appropriately active engagement. Further, the students see the reason for such engagement, just as serious piano players understand the need for endless practice at scales: the exercise may in itself seem meaningless, but the purpose of the careful drill holds their commitment.

As is so often the case, over the past several years the evidence for this need for engagement comes largely from negative findings. Students who are not deeply familiar with material cannot describe it well, cannot answer questions about it persuasively, and cannot use it in new situations. Some teachers and I sat cringing at one school, watching a respected tenth-grader called Richard who had worked hard and was expected to know the subject matter — he had memorized it as best he could — stumble when challenged or asked to analyze or use the information in a new situation. Richard had little practice with the expectation that he would really understand what was before him, deeply enough to use it beyond his immediate project. He thought he knew because he had neat lists on his project essay, but he really did not know.

Another agonizing situation arises when a student who did well on simplistic tests flounders when confronted with a demanding Exhibition. Most students in Essential schools come from elementary schools where routine tests are the norm and a more demanding (indeed, a different) standard is never applied. In Essential schools where the faculty steadfastly keeps to its objectives, the crunch for these students is unavoidable. As one ninth-grade teacher in an Essential school reported to me, "The kids are off the wall until February," when the reality of the need for serious work kicks in.[7]

When the whole routine of their classes engages students actively, two conditions usually result. The classrooms are noisier than traditional ones, full of the bustle of trial and error, of talking things through, of argument.[8] And the curriculum, in the last analysis, is a curriculum of questions (like life itself) rather than one that only requires the memorization of other people's answers to other people's questions. As I have said, this often means that the amount of subject matter that can be covered well shrinks. Thorough understanding does not come quickly. Understanding something well enough to explain and defend it in the face of reasonable but often unexpected questions requires substantial practice.[9]

We have learned that there is danger in these two consequences. A noisy classroom can be nothing more than a social gathering masquerading as collaborative work. And faced with great deficits in the ability of a group of youngsters to meet the expectation of knowing something very well and being able to use it, teachers settle for easy work. Their focus becomes simplistic Exhibitions, and the effort to prepare for them becomes a daily program that lacks the bite of serious intellectual activity. A policy of "less is more" becomes merely less.

All of us, including adolescents, learn well only when we engage. Docile kids are not engaged. To get students to concentrate productively on serious ideas requires a curriculum and an incentive system (usually tied to assessments) that attracts and involves them actively and the time required for deep mastery. Most existing schools are poorly organized to offer such conditions. Getting them to insist on such conditions is slow, often threatening work. Unless this is done, we have learned, there is no progress.[10]

5. *Human-scale places are critical.* "I cannot teach well a student whom I do not know." How many students at once can one high school teacher know well? At the start, the Coalition, somewhat arbitrarily, asserted that no teacher should have responsibility for more than 80 students. Even though the leap to this number from the more usual 100 to 180 students is heroic, the record of demonstrably successful Essential schools shows that this number is still too large.[11]

However, we have learned that there is much more to the whole matter of scale. It is not only that each teacher must have a sensible load of students. It is that the school itself has to be of human scale — a place where everyone can know everyone else. Of course, smallness is just the beginning, but it is a necessary precondition.

More than one teacher must know each child (and her family) well, and there must be time for those teachers, and, as necessary, her parents, to discuss that child. It is fine for me to know Jessica, a ninth-grader; but my knowledge of her is necessarily limited to her participation in my classes and our personal relationship. She may well be known quite differently by another teacher, who is a different person and who teaches her a different subject. Together that teacher and I and her parents can construct a fuller, fairer portrait of Jessica than any of us can alone.

Such sharing of knowledge about kids requires trusting colleague-ship among teachers. If we are hired merely on the basis of our certification areas ("secondary school U.S. and European history teacher") and seniority in the school system ("First hired, last fired"), we join a school as independent operators, are given our classrooms, and consult and collaborate only when the spirit moves us. But when we are chosen to work in a school on the basis of a commitment to the philosophy of that school and because our arrival will strengthen the corps of staff members already there, the relationship of each of us to the others is always crucial, particularly so if the school is taking on tough reforms.

How many colleagues can work effectively together? No more, our hunch is, than can attend a crowded potluck supper. So much of importance in schools depends on trust, and trust arises from familiarity and from time spent together getting divisive issues out on the table and addressing them. A team of twenty-five to thirty teachers, a number large enough for variety and small enough for trust, might be ideal. This implies, given average secondary school pupil-teacher ratios, a school of 325 to 420 pupils, itself a human-scale number. Adolescent anonymity is unlikely in such a place.

How, some protest, does one create such small units when school buildings are very large? The answer is to divide the students into small, fully autonomous units, each in effect its own school within a large "educational apartment building."[12]

What does it take to work together effectively? A mix of inspired leadership, candor, and restraint. Schools are difficult places, filled with issues over which reasonable people will disagree. A process to work the inevitable kinks out is necessary, as is the time for that process to proceed.[13]

A kid has just been caught with a pinch of marijuana; he is a first-time offender. Should we suspend him? "We need to set an example." Or do we just slap his wrist hard? "He's really scared — he needs support now."

Those English-prize essays: which is best and why? Who gets the prize? Should there be a prize? What signals, good and bad, do prizes send?

An unmarried teacher is pregnant. As she comes to term, should she continue to teach? "She models the very behavior that we must not condone." "She's a stellar teacher; the kids love her." "Her private life is her own business." "Each case deserves to be decided on its merits."

A teacher always seems to be sick exactly the number of days that the contract allows for sick leave. "He is pulling our chain." "No, he is legitimately ill."

A ninth-grader just slugged an older kid in the cafeteria. Apparently the older kid was needling him. Suspend the hitter? "Violence is not tolerated here, ever." "He was just a new kid lashing out, a first offender. No one was really hurt — go easy on him." What to do with the provoker? And who can say what the extent of the provocation was?

"That science project clearly deserved an A." "Absolutely not. The kid hasn't a clue about her topic and it shows. She is just parading what she lifted from *Science* and a *Nova* program. She deserves nothing more than a B minus." "But this is the kid's best work yet. Nothing she displayed is incorrect, and you don't know that she lifted anything."

The very existence of such confrontations, of course, makes teaching an endlessly stimulating occupation. These are real issues that affect real people every day, and they are issues as influential in people's lives as they are controversial. They can be dealt with well only in schools small enough to allow for trusting relationships among the staff and with the students.

Human scale is only the beginning. The culture of the place is also critical. Essential schools with high morale reflect the dignity deserved by teachers as well as students. The little things symbolize it well. Teachers are given not only the time to struggle with the substance and standards of the students' daily work but also the civilities of access to telephones and trust in their use. A copying machine is available for all, not just the administrative staff. There are no time clocks or check-ins. Teachers are expected to consult with one another, and easy relationships among colleagues — formal or informal, as the individuals like — are the norm. These matters are the important minutiae of schoolkeeping, the little things that send institutional signals.

Work in an Essential school (as in most others) is hard. The pressure is bearable if the work is respected, not only in word but in the way the adult community functions. Essential schools that have worked out their relationships clearly serve their students better than those in which the adults go their own ways civilly or are full of tension and disrespect.

Sensitive leaders know how to create strong and humane school cultures and when to gather collective support. The more democratically — meaning common agreement on the process for decision-making — the unit behaves, the better, or so it clearly appears to us now. The tougher the issue is, the more likely it is that collective consideration of how to deal with it will serve the school best. Dealing with critical matters takes candor, courage, and a willingness to live with the consequences of collective decisions. The leader (the principal, usually) has to know how to balance executive responsibility and the necessity of resolving pressing issues with the need to consult and develop consensus.

Good teaching requires a strong relationship between the instructor and the instructed. Learning requires a safe place, and that means not only physical and psychological safety ("I will not be mugged and I will not be humiliated") but a climate in which a student knows that he can ask any question with the assurance that a well-known adult will attend to it. A safe place is a stable place. Most of the adults there today will be there tomorrow. The students can always depend on them.

While all of this sounds obvious, the absence of human scale in many high schools is widespread. Too many schools are perceived as factory-like delivery systems rather than places to provoke deep thinking by young people about important things. Too many teachers believe that they are essentially independent operators, hired to ply their trade in an isolated classroom and to be bothered as little as possible by the school-wide community in which each classroom resides.

The evidence in favor of human-scale environments and a teacher-student ratio of one to eighty or fewer comes largely from negative findings. Some schools, however devoted to redesign, have not been able to reduce teacher loads dramatically. They thereby remain racked with faculty dissension, which paralyzes all reform beyond generalized rhetoric.[14] Big schools remain the prisoners of procedures rather than relationships to get through a day, and many of their students thus remain aloof and difficult to engage. The poor performance of such students reflects this.

The limited but growing number of small Essential schools (or small autonomous units within a larger institution) that have been able to build coherent relationships demonstrably outperform their large and bureaucratically ensnared brethren.[15]

6. *Adults must be interesting and confident.* It is possible to visit a school where all the structures are right, where the goals and visions are well codified and fully displayed, where everything seems to be functioning smoothly, yet there is no spark. It is also possible to listen to a parent excitedly describe with delight a very different place, his child's school, a place that is bereft of many amenities. The difference lies with the people at a given school, the teachers and the other adults — who they are and the relationships among them.

It has long and wisely been said that good teachers will do good work in a shed and the best-equipped building full of dull adults will fail. Students are energized by adults who are excited about what they are doing. Gusto counts. Persistence and intelligence and being informed count. Transparently loving one's subject counts. Being so sure of oneself as a scholar-teacher that one can easily and readily admit not knowing something counts. Being visibly engaged with important ideas and enthralled with a new book or mathematical proof or piece of software counts.

If adults act the way they hope the students will, the results are palpable. As before, the Coalition's evidence for this is heavy on the negative side. Teachers who feel no urgent interest in their subjects, or who have little deep understanding of their field and are too tired or overloaded or exasperated to gain such understanding, or who are so caught up in the often necessary politics of their school, send a signal to their students that the *ideas* of the work they present are not really all that important. If those ideas are not important to the adults, they are unlikely to be important to the students.

Of course, many teachers care deeply about their subjects, but the agonizing grind of their overloaded professional lives, the myriad needs of their students (only some of which relate to academic work), and the endless pulling and hauling from one budget level to another, one schedule to another, one crisis to another, ultimately become deadening. Some teachers with classroom zest are profoundly undermined by testing systems that do not demand a comparable response from students. Most of all, too few people in administration, either in the districts and above or in the unions, talk much about — and thus exhibit concern for — what it takes to be an interesting teacher. They make available constructed "professional development" rather than supporting "following one's scholarly interests," and often they institute a system of promotion that excessively rewards mere seniority.

Where teachers are full of questions about ideas, where they talk about them — heatedly argue about them — among themselves but in range of the students, the effect is real. The kids show it.[16] Where conditions reward both respectful candor and determined risk-taking, the self-styled curmudgeons, the respected traditionalists, the dedicated progressives, and the starry-eyed newcomers fresh from college all find the will and the reward in discovering more logical and thus more powerful ways of teaching.[17]

Being an interesting person connects with leadership. I know of no school so far that has "broken through" without a strong principal or team leader and a core of determined faculty members. Few schools make much progress if the demonstrably sensible plans they put forward are continually second-guessed or undermined by higher authorities. But leadership, it now strikes me, is not merely being forceful or gung-ho or simply operating where no higher authority tells one what to do. It is first and foremost being persuasive and determined about matters that count — that is, about learning and teaching and caring about kids and each other.

7. *Practice caring rigor and rigorous caring.* Many teachers work hard to catch the attention and interest of students, to get them to heed serious academic work, to make sense of their lives. As the students come to understand that these teachers care, they often turn to them, smothering them with concerns that barely touch their academic work.[18] Not surprisingly, the teachers respond; and when they have to make a tough academic call about the work of a student from a troubled situation, they often flinch. Knowing that the child is hurting inside the home, they do not want to hurt him inside the school. So they accept poorer work than the youngster can in fact produce. Then, when these

devoted school people who have served their students well in human terms run up against continued low academic performance by those kids, the frustration and the sense of betrayal — by the students and by the "system" — is poignant. They quite rightly feel that they should not be asked to carry both social and academic burdens. They feel that they are losers on both sides.[19]

One sees this in wonderfully well-intentioned schools that hold kids from low-income and often disorganized households and that serve as virtual sanctuaries for many of them. These schools meet a human need — they are "personalized" and considerate places — but their students often appear to fall short academically. Therein lies the rub: to let a student's academic work slip may put that young person terribly at risk in the long run, but pushing hard on the academic side might drive him away or greatly increase the stress in his life in the short run.

The trick for Essential schools has been to serve both ends, indeed to connect them. Being undemanding is not being caring. The greatest gift a teacher can give is to instill in students a deserved confidence in the use of their minds.

Students will not quickly or readily get this point, and we therefore come back to the need for small schools where there is enough sustained contact between each student and his teachers to allow that student to see this connection and believe in it — because he knows his teachers well enough to trust them. Flunking a test is not rejection; the low grade is primarily about the work and secondarily about the person. Poor performance tells the student and the teacher that a better performance is needed in the near future.

It is in this context that the controversial issue of tracking arises. Few successful Essential schools track — by which I mean that they do not formally assign groups of students to special sections for extended periods of time on the basis of an analysis of their competence. The evidence that tracking is a self-fulfilling prophecy (students will believe they are in fact what their teachers say they are) and serves few well is very strong.[20] However, passions remain high in favor of segregation by (presumed) ability, especially among those who believe that their children are precocious and are held back by association with less able or less motivated kids.

If tracking means that all children are pushed as hard and as appropriately as they deserve, then there must be massive tracking — every child on his or her own track. Not all children will be precocious in all subjects all the time; teachers will vary the push by child, by topic, by situation, by time. Small schools with flexible schedules and arrangements for grouping students, ones in which the students are well known, can allow for this regular and sensible adjustment. Who one sits beside and has discussions with can vary by age, ability, precocity, gender, and so on. The trick is to expect the best from everyone all the time. The record of small schools, especially small private schools, is revealing on this point.[21]

Coalition schools that have connected high expectations with personal understanding and caring have seen significant positive effects, on both students' confidence and their actual performance. Indeed, the latter creates the former.

8. *Control, autonomy, and choice are essential.* Long-established systems take poorly to those who want to change them. Essential schools force change. Essential schools that are at the prominent center of a school system — highly visible or the only high school in town — have usually had to fight inch by inch to get even a modicum of autonomy. At every step of the way, they have had to ask permission. Ironically, traditional schools in the same school system have not had to ask permission to continue with their familiar practices, even when these have been discredited in the eyes of the leaders of the system itself. The burden of proof has been entirely on the groundbreakers.

Essential schools that have had an easier time of bucking the system are those at the edges of a large district, usually serving low-income families, or those that have been publicly identified as schools of choice, or completely new schools. They are expected to be "better," "different," or they serve a population with long records of dropping out and the system gives them room if they appear to be reversing that trend.

It is easy to bash the system. When we look closely at it, however, we see few villains. The people giving permission or simply looking the other way when new (and persuasive) practices are introduced are nonetheless expected to operate the schools from the top. If they even appear to delegate their responsibilities to those lower on the bureaucratic ladder, they risk being caught up short. They remain responsible; and when something goes awry in a school, their school boards and the press turn up the heat. And the heat is ferocious. Few big-city superintendents last even five years in office.

Even within large bureaucratic systems, totally new schools can move decisively. They can recruit faculty members for their fit, in every sense. They have no closets for skeletons, no "bad" or "good" history. If they are public schools of choice or charter schools, their specialness is a virtue. The luckier ones operate under regulatory arrangements that provide sweeping permission up front. In recent years, some of these new schools have been created when excessively large high schools are closed and a cluster of small schools are put in their buildings.

The growth in interest in such fresh starts during the mid-1990s is striking — a measure, perhaps, of growing political impatience with existing hierarchical arrangements. These fresh additions to public education are not merely the alternative schools of the 1960s, destined to remain at the edges and enrolling troublesome students (or the children of obstreperous parents). They are beginning to affect the system.[22]

Choice helps in that it attracts parents who care about a particular school. The ability to choose provides an affirmation that profoundly affects the attitudes of parents and teachers and cements the alliance for thoughtful and hard work by all involved. Whether these schools of choice are in the public or the private sector appears to make little difference.

The record of Essential schools such as those described at the end of each chapter in this book reflects these realities. Of the schools that have been able to break through, a disproportionate number have been new or fundamentally redesigned existing schools. Such a finding is obviously disappointing. We hoped that the existing apparatus for school government could in fact strenuously press forward with significant reform.

9. *Attempting too little is a recipe for failure.* The record clearly shows that meaningful changes in the performance of students and in the stability of their school rarely take place when that school attends to only one or two of the common elements that characterize an Essential

school.[23] Asking the students to be more active without changing the schedule or insisting on significant Exhibitions, for example, usually leads nowhere. Active engagement, such as a demanding science project, takes time, and the forty-seven-minute period provides little time.

Asking the students to write more and to meet a higher standard for their writing will not work if teachers still carry loads of 130 or more students. A focused and deep curriculum that is interdisciplinary when sensible rarely flourishes if externally imposed tests follow old patterns of sweeping and thus superficial coverage. Teaching each student "where he is" meshes poorly with most age grading and tracking patterns. And, as we have seen, urging — much less insisting — that teachers and administrators change their practice has little effect unless combined with resources and patience.[24]

A little change is no change at all. Gradual reform might be easier in the short run, but it serves the ultimate goal badly. Everything important in a school affects everything else, and if synergy among the key elements is not achieved, the result is frustration. Essential schools that take the gradual approach appear to be having a harder time of reform than those that are able to charge ahead with a comprehensive plan.[25]

10. *Start as early as possible.* Habits of all kinds are set early. The sooner a child can get into good school habits, the better. Those Essential schools that start with sixth- or seventh-graders — in effect, junior-senior high schools — appear to have an easier time of it than those that start with ninth- or tenth-graders. Those with a full pathway — preschool through high school — are most promising.[26]

11. *The relationship between the top and the bottom of the educational hierarchy must be fundamentally rethought.* Our experience with the governance of schools has led to four principal conclusions. First, stability of leadership within the system is crucial. Schools endlessly affected by changes — new superintendents, each with a new plan; new governors, also with "new initiatives"; new legislative leadership — are pulled in frustratingly different directions. We have seen school principals and teachers figuring out practically, and often cynically, how to

fend off the worst of any new order, knowing that this year's innovation may well not be operative next year.

Term limits for elected officers are a curse for educators. Elected officials are here today, gone tomorrow. As a consequence, the system is run by civil servants, people who are usually protected by tenure and who quite understandably have a special stake in the status quo. Political volatility and the resulting power of the more permanent bureaucracy do have their good points, however: Essential schools that have strong and influential supporters within the bureaucracy can quietly flourish whatever the policy rhetoric might be at any given moment.

The point remains that serious school reform requires steady and consistent support and a great deal of patience. A "here today, gone tomorrow" political system makes the necessary continuity extremely difficult to achieve.

Second, the way the policy community and the bureaucracy view schooling is crucial. If the metaphor of the bloodless assembly line persists, little change happens. Dealing with children in the aggregate ("all the eighth-graders in this state," "all children from families below the poverty line") and perceiving each child as an individual ("just like each of my own very different children") lead policy in very different directions. The latter, obviously — as it reflects reality — is preferable.

Policymakers, of course, have to view the large scene, but they do not have to reduce that scene to crude generalities. Accepting both the diversities implicit in schooling — the differences among children, neighborhoods, and professionals — and the need to attend carefully to the wishes, commitments, and proper rights of parents makes system policy and practice complex, and thus a nuisance. We have found that when the subtleties are honored and when there has been bipartisan commitment to a reform direction, the results are promising.[27]

In 1988, the Coalition of Essential Schools formally allied with the Education Commission of the States (an association of state governments for collective study of educational policy and practice) in a project dubbed Re:Learning to pursue what we called a strategy of reform "from the schoolhouse to the statehouse." The assumption here was that the governmental "top" and the school-level "bottom" would work as close allies, with the demands and particular needs of the bottom — the individual schools — profoundly shaping the top's specific policies.

Over the past years some fifteen states have been involved, directly or indirectly, in this project, which has led to efforts to bring together the teaching and policy communities for greater understanding of each other's roles (gatherings rarely held in previous times), state assignment of staff to support Essential schools and kindred reforming schools, state funds to support the reform, and waivers of regulations to give the schools room to redesign their work. In several states this activity has led to reform legislation — specific support to risk-taking schools. Most important, Re:Learning has given legitimacy to the work of those schools trying to break with unwise practices. The informed blessing of the top has provided substantial support for the bottom, as the rapid growth of Essential schools after 1988 evidences.

Third, leaders at both the top and the bottom have to understand that managing a school is rather like sailing a boat. There is a chart, there is a planned course, and there are plotted shoals and sandbars, but those on board have to adjust all the time to changing winds and tides, even redrawing the course to the destination from time to time. There are goals for a school and a framework of expectations for how those goals may be reached, but the means, and even the framework itself, are subject to constant adjustment on the basis of what is going on with the children, the staff, and the community. The hand of government has to be a light one, and a trusting one. Directing the sailboat from an office ashore is as imprudent as directing the activities of an individual school from a school system's central headquarters.

Finally, respect and sustained, genuine communication between top and bottom are essential. Where there are differences, they should be addressed. Too often they are swept under a rug while the state or district tries to ram its views home and the locals sit on their hands, griping.

Of course, the conventional wisdom implies that higher government has the right to overrule lower government. The fact that these "levels" of government arise more from the realities of scale (towns are smaller than states) and from political arrangements than from citizens' rights obscures the fact that the compulsory nature of public education puts an enormous responsibility for restraint on governmental leaders. Some give that responsibility too little respect, with predictable resentment and opposition at the bottom.

The shape and obligations of all the pieces of the public school system as we know it are under fresh scrutiny. State and city leaders' willingness to contemplate radical changes in that system is strikingly more prevalent today than when the Coalition's work started. The system is under criticism unprecedented in this century. We hope that the new forms it takes adhere carefully to the convictions represented by Re:Learning's slogan, *"from* the schoolhouse *to* the statehouse."

12. *Clusters of schools proceed more effectively than schools alone.* The Coalition in its early years was a group of individual schools, each making its own way in its own setting. As the numbers of schools grew, for administrative convenience we organized regional centers to provide the kind of support usually delivered from the Coalition's central office at Brown University. We have since realized that clustering has important substantive virtues.

The schools play off against one another, comparing work, consulting on new directions, promoting honest talk by faculty members across schools, serving each other as sustained "critical friends." A cluster of schools can help others in their midst get started, both through the small staffs they hire and by lending veteran teachers as consultants.

The schools protect one another politically. In one extraordinary instance, a new district superintendent threatened to fire a principal because she had raised substantial moneys on her own for her school's library, which made it far richer than comparable libraries in nearby schools. The superintendent found this inequitable; no school should have a much bigger library than others. The principal had to cease this fund-raising, he ordered. Principals at the other schools in the cluster and the cluster's staff had contacts with the local newspaper, and the story quickly reached page one. The superintendent backed off. Entrepreneurial energy was applauded and the poverty of school library budgets was exposed.

In some places, such as in New York City, clusters in fact operate in some respects as formal school districts. They collectively prepare standards and expectations for Exhibitions, and they make the work of their students public. They monitor and support one another. When it is efficient, they make collective purchases. They have negotiated with the state for collective waivers of regulations. They are professional and governmental units in all but name. They profoundly redefine what is meant by the top and the bottom.

13. *Respect the persistent tortoise.* From its start, the Coalition of Essential Schools has been criticized for its (deliberate) vagueness — its direction is plotted only by means of a set of generally worded convictions — and for its comprehensiveness — it assumes that for reform to count, the school must be addressed as a whole, with all its aspects up for consideration. The burdens on the people at the school site for creating a design and implementing it in all its complexity are therefore substantial.

We knew from the start, from our own personal experience, that progress would be tortuous and slow. The people at each school would have to recreate their work in a manner authentic in their particular setting. They would have to sell that new school to their constituencies. They would have to take the time necessary to translate the new plans into practice. Impatient people wanting measurable results would be continually disappointed. Given the difficulty of the work, critics would find that progress was "uneven" — this being meant as hostile criticism. Traditional educational oxen would be gored, and as a result, controversy in many places would be rife. Some schools would never get their work off the ground. Others would not survive counterrevolutions.

All of this was expected because the Essential school effort is both comprehensive and by its nature unsettling. It takes determined, tough-minded folk to tackle the work.

Given this difficult road to travel and the weak incentives to do so, why has the Coalition grown in numbers of schools involved, at an ever accelerating rate? There may be three explanations.

One is that the commonsense shape of the project does strike a chord with experienced school people and those who listen to them. These people know, for example, that one cannot teach 150 children well at once and that confronting that issue, with all of its rippling side effects, is necessary, whatever the pain. They know that high schools are different from primary schools, that the character and substance of standards for adolescents must be profoundly different from those outlined for young children, and that designing these standards will force substantial changes in school practice, even in how school people, children, and parents define "standards."

Paradoxically, perhaps, the comprehensiveness of Essential school work and its insistence that each design reflect local circumstances are persuasive precisely because they are demanding. Experienced school people and policymakers know that simple or categorical approaches to school reform have not worked and will not work. They know that the typical high school today is profoundly misdesigned and that all the pieces of that design fundamentally interconnect. They know that an effort to address that reality, however painful, must be made, and that to do so in partnership with others — within a coalition — can serve them well.

The second reason arises from the promise represented in the history of those schools that have been at Essential work for a decade and that have been able to address Horace's compromises. With all their messiness and often difficult political history, they bear witness that schools can be changed, and profoundly so, and that children can do better than what everyone expected them to do. The Coalition no longer has to make its argument in the abstract. There are now a number of exemplars to signal its efficacy. It can be done.

Finally, the localism of the effort is appealing. There is respect here: the assumption is that those close to the children ultimately know what is best for them. Wise local folk reach out to others working on similar problems. There is no point in entirely reinventing the wheel, and there is political safety in numbers, especially in collective evaluations of the work of all the schools. The Coalition is often called primarily a *conversation,* serious talk among honest people about serious common work. It is not something delivered from on high. Strong people respond to that, especially as they know well that standardized solutions affecting diverse communities result in mediocre work, or worse.

Serious people also know that the way to new high schools will be slow and arduous, that there will not be quick results, that the early days of the work may be filled more with controversy than with unchallenged progress. The record of the successful early Essential schools tells this story well and also tells the story of ultimate breakthroughs. It would be nice if the reform of secondary schooling could proceed with the speed of a running hare. The record, however, suggests the persistent tortoise.

These thirteen findings — hunches and more — are hardly surprising. The practices they represent stand the test of common sense as well as that of experience. The frustration for Essential school people is that introducing these practices is often very difficult.

Obvious though these findings are, they highlight a reality for most serious contemporary school reform: that students are more likely to accrue success from the culture of their school — its clear convictions and the way in which those convictions are honored in practice — than from its formal technical structure. Good structures (such as enough time to do important work in class) are needed, for obvious reasons, but what the students do within those structures is what counts. That doing rests on the attitudes and confidence of the school's staff — indefinable, fleeting qualities, ones as impossible to mandate as they are important. That fact makes large-scale school reform profoundly difficult.

The attitudes and commitments and relationships among a school's faculty, its students, and its parents are crucial. Without these, the best-laid plans for Exhibitions, flexible schedules, advisory periods, and the rest of the familiar paraphernalia of Coalition practice and that of similar reform efforts come to very little.

Flexible and appropriate school and system structures are important. A steady and supportive district and state are important. Without them, dedicated teachers cannot turn their commitments into action. But the game of serious education ultimately rests with powerful teachers, supportive parents, and determined students. Finding the way to gather these people together is the heart of the matter, the ultimate systemic reform. Above all else, that is what matters.

◆ *New Practice from New Evidence*

"Our mission is to hook them in through rigor." The speaker is Nancy Mohr, the principal of a small school housed in a building on the campus of Bronx Community College in New York City. The "them" are students who have dropped out or drifted through New York City's high schools, finding no place to stick, no place where they are inspired to buckle down and learn. Some come to University Heights High School as a last resort; some come in choosing a better way. However, they have to work hard even to get in.

I watched the interview of a prospective candidate, conducted by a panel of students and faculty. The examining students were mostly older than I expected — some were in their late teens — and some of the faculty members were less than a decade older than their charges. They, the setting, and their style were informal — jeans, sweatshirts, nondescript furniture, coffee cups, nothing carefully lined up in rows. The tone was respectful, however, at times even austere. The applicant was treated as an adult. This getting into school was serious business, and the assumption was that the applicants were serious people. The signal to the candidate I watched was clear: leave the attitude at the door. Given the street experience of the candidates, seriousness is probably a way of life for them, but they surely have rarely seen it reflected in school.

The committee's task was a complicated one. Should the young man before them be allowed to enter? The criteria were simple. Would he work hard? Would he keep clean of drugs? Would he never engage in threats or violence? Would he tell the truth? Would he show up and do his work, religiously? Would he, above all, *try?*

University Heights High School enrolls some 400 students, 60 percent Latino and 40 percent African American. Most are from low-income families. Assuming that a candidate persuades the committee that he will try, school starts with an assessment of where his academic world is and goes from there. He graduates only when he presents a portfolio detailing his command of seven interdisciplinary domains, which involve the traditional academic areas. A three-thousand-word letter must introduce this work. Again a committee presides, this time with many outsiders, drawn from the Bronx community, parents of University Heights students, teachers from other schools and the community college, and friends from the Coalition of Essential Schools and kindred groups.

The students' efforts are focused on these seven domains and a set of specific skills. Each student's program is tailor-made, a necessity given the crazy quilt of backgrounds from which the students come. The school is organized around teams of some 130 students and 8 teachers; the teams stay together all day, in effect forming small schools. The review — exhibition — of work comes frequently, in what the school calls Roundtables. Every student's effort is on view; there is no hiding here, academically or personally.

The faculty talk is engaging. It is endlessly about the students. What does she know? Where is she, a Spanish-speaker, in English? Is she lying? If so, why? Is it something about us that forces her to lie? Does she want to be out of here? Why? Is that work good enough? Does that project require enough from him? Will it show us that he really can do good work? And tell us, please God, what good work is!

The school twists and turns. It is absolutely rigid when it comes to violence and abuse — you do it, you're out — and adaptive in all other ways, cajoling good work from young adults who have never before seen it, much less produced it. The work requires endless patience. Students are skeptical, wary of the officialdom that is a public school.

They like the ambiance of a college campus, but most know when they arrive that they have miles to go before they can be real college students.

The twists and turns work. Fewer than 3 percent of those who are admitted drop out. Over 92 percent of those who graduate gain college admission, and most who get there survive.

Are the graduates typical graduates? In many ways yes, and in many ways no. They still have the toughness with which they arrived, often a striking and admirable quality. Many are parents. Some earn their own keep. Their resilience shows, as does the character of their accomplishment. These are admirable young people, steeled by growing up harshly, and their success glistens.

University Heights High School, Bronx, New York; Nancy Mohr, principal. Member of the Coalition of Essential Schools since 1987.

6

Troublesome Complexities

UNDERNEATH the intense talk about public schooling lie some fundamental complexities so substantial and unsettling that they are rarely mentioned in the formal debate about reform and thus only rarely (and then furtively) addressed in practice. They must be pondered, carefully. They are too important to sidestep. They will not go away.

In formal debate, for example, there is an implicit assumption that Americans agree about the purposes of education. We can have national or state standards because, it is assumed, there is a basic consensus about the ends of schooling. Or, more pessimistically expressed, our leaders believe that such a basic consensus must be pushed upon a careless public.

For the elementary school level, this assumption may be reasonable. Americans want their children to be able to read, write, and cipher. They want them to understand how their culture works. They want them to enjoy learning. They want them to be decent, healthy people. They want them to be prepared to get and hold good jobs. When one goes beyond these ends, questions emerge.

Once while meeting informally during the summer, three old educator friends and I talked for a day about the condition of the national teachers' unions, how and where they fit effectively into the school reform effort, and how their definition might thus substantially alter.

Inevitably, in time we got on to what the schools were ultimately about. How could we talk of teachers' unions without having a clear assumption about the purpose of their members' craft? I was asked to sum up my hopes for high school graduates' education in a crisp phrase. *Informed skepticism,* I replied. The answer set off a wonderfully roiling conversation.

Skepticism? Kids have to know something before they can be responsibly skeptical. The country needs agreement on things among its people. Common schools are about bringing people together. A culture cannot operate unless it has a common vocabulary, and that must simply be imposed. Smart people over millennia have pondered the important ideas that gird our culture, and young people have the duty — the privilege — of learning from their thinking.

A common vocabulary? Who decides what it is? Will it be the same in Zuni, New Mexico, as it is in Atlanta, Georgia? Or will there be important differences as well as commonalities between places? Is it all right to have — indeed, to tolerate, even to encourage — such differences? Will the effort to create a common vocabulary by means of law be deeply resented, even fuel serious, legitimate protest?

America is an amalgam of diverse cultures. The common school is the entity making that amalgam possible.

Nonsense. Whether we like it or not, the media are the new amalgam, astonishingly powerful and getting more so. We Americans have today a common consumerist amalgam. What we need are basic schools that countervail that powerful and basically undemocratic force, places that teach kids to be skeptical of the myriad messages that are dished up for them.

We must stay the course, with government setting the goals. Otherwise the quality will go. We have to have standards. We must insist on standards.

Standards for what? Sure, kids should know many things, have many skills. But crucial to them all must be the adolescents' attitude toward those things. It should be an attitude of questioning. The students must habitually ask, "Why is this so? What if it were to be addressed in a different way? What isn't there? How can I find that out?" Knowledge without skepticism is knowledge waiting to be distorted.

The result will be chaos.

No, the result will mirror the real world, the real world of serious scholarship as well as the world of the street, the family, and the workplace.

Lots of people will be afraid of this. They want kids to recognize and respond well to authority. They want their children to believe what they believe. We want our kids to respect, say, the Constitution. Or the biblical explanation for the advent of human life.

I want them to respect it because they have explored it in their own informed way and found the belief persuasive.

Our conversation ran on, and could have run on for hours more. What I learned was how much honest disagreement there is about the ends of a serious secondary education — what lies beyond the rudiments — and how that disagreement existed among four good friends who collectively had more than 130 years of professional school experience. We did agree, however, on one thing: that whatever was ultimately decided on in these matters — a goal of informed skepticism or something else — it would profoundly affect the design and culture of a school and school system.

The discussion we had was rare, perhaps because it was and is so unsettling. It is easier simply to get on with the familiar, with deciding the standards in, say, high school English, or designing Exhibitions for kids to display their learning. It is far harder and certainly more painful to step back and ask what all this is for in the first place.

There is evidence that the slow progress of any kind of change in American schools over the past few decades is a result of a tacit acceptance of differences among stated goals. Planning some change will force troubling issues of the kind we discussed out into the open, giving light to our differences. Letting the sleeping dog of existing practices lie assures that it will not wake up and make us pay attention.

The dissatisfaction expressed in many quarters about the recently drafted voluntary national standards in various school subjects, most vocally over those affecting American history, is evidence of disagreement. Even more so is the general lack of interest in this standard-setting effort. The work finds itself in the public eye only when there is some juicy controversy to report.

We can find further evidence of the depth of disagreement in the accelerating public interest in having choice in the public school sector. If a family can choose the school that reflects the culture it most prefers, there simply will not be a *common* school. Families will choose among schools. Such a situation would represent a major shift in Americans' belief about public education. The momentum behind such a change is coming from all across the political spectrum, although it is never articulated in quite this way. It presents us with discomfiting complexity.

Equally discomfiting are the implications for schooling of emerging research on the nature and means of human learning, work that puts new pressure on familiar formulas about learning and thereby about cultivating the mind. These are not matters of philosophical hair-splitting. They rest on substantial evidence.[1]

One of the most familiar teacherly metaphors is that of building blocks. A student learns this and then this and then this, in a careful sequence. He does arithmetic before algebra; he can't even sniff the tantalizing aromas of the latter until he has a working mastery of the basic arithmetic procedures. He may not discuss the issue of gun ownership until he has thoroughly covered the Constitution. He cannot play Mozart until he is adept at scales.

The metaphor appears sensible, until we recall how we ourselves learn. From our own experience, we know that we learn when we think, the harder the better. We even reduce that important conclusion to a familiar expression: when confronted with a better answer to a question than we had before, we say, "Oh, I didn't think of that."

We think hard both when the issue at hand is inherently interesting — that is, when we are motivated to learn — and when we see that issue in a relatively familiar context. For example, we do not fully understand how zero works in arithmetic unless we use the concept in an algebraic context. We do not "get" the Second Amendment unless we tangle with a case such as gun ownership. We do not proceed with our flute practice if the sounds we produce, when accurate, have no pleasing melody. Likewise, we cannot do algebra without arithmetic concepts, or fathom the gun issue without a fair sense of constitutional principles, or play Mozart on the flute without the physical disciplines of breath and fingering. The metaphor of strictly defined building blocks, each addressed in isolation and in strict sequence, is clearly unsatisfactory.

We learn when we want to learn and when what is to be learned is embedded in a relatively familiar context. Scholars call this "situated learning."[2] We learn by making repeated rushes at a concept, each time gaining a better grasp of its meaning and eventually understanding it.

There is plenty for a little child to learn about and from the very idea of "zero," and there is much that the most advanced student can learn about the same mathematical phenomenon. People learn to write when they have something worth writing: for a little child it is a thank-you note to her grandma; for the teenager it is an editorial for the school newspaper. Only in such contexts do issues of clarity and coherence become important and useful to the learner. Further, people retain the power of those concepts by continually using them in real life — that is, more letters to Grandma, more essays for the newspaper, each one more pleasing and effective. Learning is a spiral, repeated use of what are in the end very sophisticated understandings in ever more demanding contexts or situations.[3]

There is plenty of memory work and drill and practice in this process. However, these familiar recitals make sense only to the extent that they enforce and reinforce deep thinking about ideas in context. A person drills hard because he sees the point of all that effort. He drills because he has been persuaded by a respected instructor that the work is necessary, that it leads to some important place. He drills because the situation clearly calls for it, and the excitement inherent in that situation carries him along. He endlessly practices putting to prepare for a golf match or French words shortly before leaving for Quebec.

This recognition has immense implications for the curriculum, and for the very way in which a school looks at its charge. No effective school will simply march through some list of that which is presumed to be elementary toward that which is agreed to be more complex. Learning is more complicated — and, paradoxically, simpler — than that. The Harvard researcher David Perkins has summed it up in what he calls Theory One: "People learn much of what they have a reasonable opportunity and motivation to learn."[4] To be motivated, they usually have to see the work entailed as part of a larger and desired context. And the student has to be given the setting, the time, and the tools — and the teachers — to get the work accomplished.

It is all so obvious, but often so little honored in the way high schools currently function, with their swift march over lists of topics and material, which are unconnected with any understandable context and which assume that students should never be allowed to run before they are fully credentialed walkers. Rather, the learner's place — her situation — always has to be taken into account. Key ideas must be visited and revisited, in ever more demanding forms.

Accomplishing this will take far more planning and local adaptation than is currently provided for in most American high schools. We are stuck with the notion that a curriculum is primarily a list, one that applies equally well to all children in all places. There are universals, of course (clear expository prose is no different in Portland, Oregon, from good prose in Portland, Maine). But the evidence about the importance of situations — contexts that make sense to each student, one by one — and the need to circle back again and again with key ideas as each student requires, implies that the bottom level of education, the classroom, must be seen far more than it is as the cradle of the curriculum, rather than merely a place for its execution.

This finding is clearly a nuisance. Situation-free curricula are easier to design than a system that depends on substantial student-level adaptation. Unfortunately, we are stuck with the variety of our adolescents and the places where they live. The sooner we acknowledge that inconvenience and learn how to live with it, the better our students' performance will be.

At its best, the building-block metaphor represents the obvious fact that some ideas and intellectual operations are more complex, abstract, or difficult than others. Too often, however, educators believe that advanced work is simply more elementary work. Little kids know about Columbus. Middle-sized kids know about Columbus and Montezuma. Big kids know all about these two and Castro and NAFTA too.

However, the matter is not this simple. Start with the youngster who does well in a spelling bee (she spells "asthma" correctly). That is fine, but it does not get her very far. She has to learn to write simple sentences, with the words spelled correctly ("Asthma makes it hard to breathe"). Still this doesn't get her very far. She has to have something of greater and more personal consequence about which to write. The matter now transcends language; she has to describe that something clearly enough so another person can understand what she means.

If the topic can be dealt with easily, the demand is low ("I named my cat Muffie"). Demand gets higher when abstraction is added ("My father hates cats, even my fluffy Muffie") or if an explanation is necessary ("My father hates cats, including Muffie, because they make him sneeze"), or, eventually, if the student writes an essay on "who has the greater right to decide whether Muffie stays in the family, I, who love her, or my father, whose asthma is triggered when Muffie is around?" Finally, there is style, crafting the words (all still spelled correctly and arranged in comprehensible form) in such a way that the strong human feeling of the confrontation between cat and lungs — an utterly trivial confrontation unless one is personally involved — is conveyed in the recital. Style is not simply achieved from more work at the old things, spelling bees that now demand a rendering of "pyelonephrosis." The matter here is new.

I saw this condition dramatically illustrated at a magnet high school for the arts. The session was a master class, two hours long, held in a cluttered but acoustically perfect performance room.

On entering, I joined forty students who were sitting in rows arced around a grand piano, a chair, and a music stand. In the chair sat a stolid youngster probably fifteen years old, sent to this school by her parents for artistic finishing. Her hair was crammed under a Boston Red Sox cap. Her cello leaned against her jeans, and she fiddled with the strings. She scowled. Circling around her was the master, speaking softly about the Haydn piece she had chosen to play. "Now, play," he said. The accompanist started off, and some passages of the C-Major Sonata filled the room. To my ear it sounded flawless.

"Excellent, excellent," said the master calmly. "Again."

Again. And again. The thirty-nine other students watched quietly. They knew that soon they would be in that chair, bringing their hours and hours of practice to the test.

"This time, with some more *feeling*," the master pleaded. Again. The master scolded, explained: "There are thousands of good cellists and a few great artists. Do you want *only* to be a good cellist?" He leaned over the student. She remained unmoved, looking at the floor. "Again." The master got more frustrated. "Again. *Feel* the music." He took to the piano, tried demonstrating the difference between the merely technical and the truly moving.

The girl persisted, unsmiling, visibly as emotionless as the master was effusively emotional. He finally stopped. He swept close to her and asked, "Who in this room do you love? It's Valentine's Day!" A sparkle of embarrassment crossed the girl's face: "I don't know." The master persisted. She finally pointed at another young woman. The master seized a folding chair, plunked it in front of and close to the cellist, instructed the friend to sit in it, removed the music stand, and demanded, "Play to *her* — play so that it speaks to *her!*"

With a suppressed giggle, the young cellist played again. It sounded the same, technically perfect. "Again," commanded the master. A bit more of a smile emerged. She was trying hard, visibly now. Some shape came to the notes, a shape beyond the technical, even to novice ears like mine. It was subtle, but it was there. The music began to transcend the notes. Even to an amateur's ear, it had a coherence, a feeling that the notes alone failed to provide.

"Aha!" exclaimed the master. "Again," he commanded, and his young cellist could see his smile.

Higher learning is not just more of the same. It is more, surely, but there are new elements, new standards, new grace, new imagination, new commitments. The young cellist had long ago won the musical equivalent of the spelling bee and could perform with great technical precocity, but the step from that to communication with meaning was a giant one, one that required tools beyond those developed by hard and dutiful work. The new plateau to which the master was encouraging her was not just the next block up. It was a level of a different character, although it required technical expertise to reach it. I sensed that the cellist by the end *understood* the music, grasped a meaning beyond its mere composition. In so doing, she gave it life.

This young musician was demonstrably talented, and she probably came from a family and a setting where very hard work and very demanding performances were expected. That makes her special. That is a pity. The lesson from the master class for all secondary education should not be dismissed for many reasons — including the shape of a high standard that transcended "more of the same" to point to something very individual, an expression of personal understanding and subtlety, which characterizes qualities (whether in music or science or athletics or community service) that most parents dearly want to find in each of their own children.

We can find analogies to this example in other fields. The Westinghouse science competitions. The history essays written by secondary school students that are published in *The Concord Review*.[5] The superb debate team. The fine school literary magazine. The resourceful community service worker. The devoted athlete. The hot-shot chess team. High achievement, higher than expected for adolescents, is all around us. It can be provoked in many — indeed, most — young people.

If schools accept such a goal, they have to arrange for it and value it. Valuing it means building the expectation into assessment. Exhibitions must demand evidence that a high school student can not only derive meaning from something unfamiliar but approach it and communicate about it in ways that reflect the subtlety the topic deserves. That means going deep, raising the standard, circling almost endlessly around, finding the essence of the matter — even something as elusive as the feeling of a Haydn sonata.

These things are difficult to describe. One has to witness the kind of understanding and style that the hard-working cellist's experience suggests. To achieve it — even to display it — takes time, on everyone's part. Just because these goals are elusive in their sophistication, however, does not mean that schools should ignore them. Quite the contrary. Deep understanding and style should be hallmarks of any serious high school.

Few schools yet do this. No state system begins to approach it, even rhetorically. Most policymakers feel that this standard is inappropriate or too demanding or impossible to achieve, or, in its subtlety, effete. Or they ignore it because it is so difficult to test. And so they settle for spelling bees ("By God, we will at least get these right!") and rarely wonder what sort of situations would encourage more than a few American youngsters to the level of commitment and accomplishment of that cellist.

What is involved here is a standard of understanding little appreciated either in school practice or in public policy. It begs for emphasis. All adolescents should have the fullest possible chance to enjoy it. How to put it high on our list of objectives makes us anxious. This sort of standard does not readily fit.[6]

Horace Smith knows from his own experience the wonderful variety among students, a variety that changes almost daily. Adolescents, like us all, have different personalities, hopes, fears, senses of humor, ways of expressing themselves, means of understanding things and telling us what they understand. What makes them especially fun is that they often accentuate these qualities, even grotesquely. The Class Clown, the Mad Scientist, the Jock Hero, the Valley Girl, the Shadow (never really noticed), and the Mouse live (unintentionally, perhaps) in bold relief, and these stereotypic appellations barely do them justice. Adolescents are as complicated as the rest of us. Many have yet to learn how to mask their feelings or manipulate them with sophisticated subtlety to affect others. They wear their variety on their sleeves.

Horace knows that these youngsters are not all the same and should not be taught as though they were the same. Science knows this too, and the work of developmental psychologists over the past twenty-five years seriously challenges the way that high schools have traditionally functioned: largely on the basis of age. What is now better understood is the nature of the differences among us, including differences in how we learn, how we understand, how we express ourselves. These differences are not just points on a single hierarchy ("He's not that far along"). They portray different ways of knowing and expressing. While people are now arguing about whether these differences are genetic or environmental, the fact for school people is that they are there. To ignore them is to miseducate many young people.

The developmental psychologist Howard Gardner has pondered the nature of intelligence — what he calls "human intellectual competencies" — and concludes that there are probably several kinds of intelligence among the population. "A human intellectual competence must entail a set of skills of problem solving" Gardner writes, "enabling the individual *to resolve genuine problems or difficulties* that he or she encounters and, when appropriate, to create an effective product — and must also entail the potential for *finding or creating problems* — thereby laying the groundwork for the acquisition of new knowledge." Intelligence is not, then, just what is measured by IQ tests: it is something with observable consequences. When those consequences are carefully observed, different patterns of intellectual competence emerge — what Gardner calls "sets of know-how." He has identified seven. People think and learn and express themselves in a variety of ways. Attentive parents and teachers have seen it happen.[7]

Other strands of research have added knowledge to commonsense observation. There are differences in school behavior and performance between males and females, among children from different cultural and linguistic traditions and home situations. There are variations in intellectual and social development over the span of childhood through adolescence. And there is more, a torrent of information, most of which challenges the ways and means of familiar schooling, with its dependence above all else on age to grade students, on one kind of examinations to categorize them into tracks, and on one kind of teaching materials and one approach to teaching them.

We learn in different ways, and we must therefore be taught in different ways. How to accomplish this as a practical matter is a difficult issue. If addressing the varieties of human learning displayed by our students is important, schools will have to invest in knowing each student well and insist on having flexibility to act on what is known about each pupil. The adaptability seen in an effective kindergarten needs to find its way into the high school — especially given the probable greater range of differences (given the passage of years) among teenagers than among their younger siblings.

If the schools do not make this sort of accommodation, the quality of the work of some children — perhaps the majority — will seriously suffer. If the objective of secondary education includes a high standard for all children, the practical consequences of such accommodations must be faced.

Most high schools divide their work into "subjects," most commonly titled English, social studies, mathematics, science, foreign language, art, music, and so on. However, the situations that both garner the interest of adolescent learners and provide them with rich intellectual challenge, Horace knows from experience, rarely fall neatly within the boundaries of these traditional subject matters.

For example, is a problem in computing a community's real public debt an exercise in mathematics, or economics, or civics (or even politically adroit fiction writing)? Is understanding the human immune system and AIDS a lesson only in biology, or is it important to students because of the social significance or the likelihood of the spread of HIV (which draws on skills and content in both geography and statistics)?

Most human problems spread across the traditional academic domains, often in confusing and conflicting ways. Their inevitable complexity confounds adolescent minds or, more often, leads students — and their teachers and the writers of their textbooks — to simplistic conclusions.

For several centuries, scholars have evolved what are now called academic disciplines to help them understand the nature of the physical world and the world of abstraction, of ideas. Disciplines provided some order in what was otherwise chaos, different ways to view the universe. They were not sitting in nature waiting to be discovered. Rather, they were invented, and their shape and character are always in motion. In effect, they are constantly being reinvented.

Many metaphors have been used to describe the disciplines. They are lenses to examine phenomena. They are the trunks of trees from which extend a variety of branches. They are mechanisms which, when dutifully followed, allow for consistent and thereby comparable forms of inquiry. They are clusters of ideas, evolved in an agreed-upon manner, which provide a common substance, a set of experiences that can be shared.

Disciplines are often confused with subject matters. The two necessarily overlap, in obvious ways. "Subject matter," as frequently defined by school people, refers simply to a lump of gathered material. History is the facts about what happened in the past. Mathematics is numbers and their manipulation. English is words and stories and plays. The more of these things we have grasped, the better we are. Differently put, subject matter is data about human and physical existence arranged in a rational, orderly way.

The word "discipline," however, implies use, the application of ideas arising from subject matter in particular ways, using particular methods. Matter is inert — until used. "Covering the discipline's material" does not necessarily provoke the use of the discipline; merely reading *A Farewell to Arms* and knowing its plot does not necessarily lead to a grasp of how to make sense of — that is, to understand — a creative written work. If a student is never asked to gain this grasp — that is, to practice the discipline — he gets no practice in making sense of something with which he might be confronted in the future, such as a new piece of fiction. Subject matter is yin to the disciplinary yang; both the stuff of knowledge and the means to use it creatively are required.

However, this is too neat. The stuff of learning — the subject matter — is the yield of endless creative use, the ideas, evidences, and frames of reference that develop from experience. The stuff, then, is itself in constant motion, not just because fashions change (witness the slightly shifting points of view that affect the choice of details in history texts over time) but because humankind, to put it simply, is always learning more or learning differently or learning better. Serious ideas, both the fruit of inquiring experience and the basis for further inquiry, never stand still.

The extremes prove the rule. Some things are facts: on a totally windless day, drop a ball bearing from the top of the Empire State Building and it will fall down toward the street. Some things are convictions: there is an afterlife. Experience cannot prove this, even though in some form it may be true. Most matters of consequence fall in the middle. The subject matters are fungible, to be treated with both respect and skepticism. How one treats them is the discipline.

In the practical world of today's schools, what are the disciplines? What are the subject matters? By and large, we dodge these questions, preferring to stay with familiar formulations. As one respected scholar now involved in school reform recently said to me, we don't have time to address these issues. The momentum of the old ways and the realization that addressing them will provoke an academicians' battle royal turn our attention away.

The English teacher Horace Smith, whose work is profoundly affected by these matters, is thus stuck with the status quo — in the way his work is categorized and organized, in the way in which his students are assessed — even though research universities are redefining and thereby deepening the subject matters and disciplines that are at the heart of their scholarship. What is "English" is up for grabs in the academy. In most high schools, however, English is what English was. The costs to Horace and to Horace's students are heavy.

Twenty years ago the historian Lawrence A. Cremin delivered a prescient series of lectures at Columbia University, carefully suggesting that educational policy should deliberately attend to what he called "configurations" of education, by which he meant the creative and effective weaving together of several agencies of deliberate education — the public school, public television, the churches, and organized youth activities, among others.[8] He argued that we should stop equating learning with schooling only, that young people have always learned, intentionally or incidentally, whether well or not, from a variety of influences, and that we should acknowledge that simple reality. Cremin urged Americans to think comprehensively about education, to put together the aspects of the culture that could be effectively brought to bear on young people's learning, and to arrange things so that such resources would be absolutely public vehicles for equality of opportunity and social cohesion. He meditated on the varied, often clashing claims of the individual and the community as a whole and implied that a sensitive congeries of educating institutions could protect the interests of both.

Twenty years after Cremin's lectures, the power of the nonschool educating influences has increased astonishingly, largely through the advent of digital technology and its application in telecommunications and computing. Cremin's argument is more important today even than it was in 1975; indeed, it is crucial. The existing high school is shrinking in its influence precisely because the competition for adolescents' minds and hearts has grown so powerful. The fact that the existing secondary school clings to its old ways compounds the problem.

To create a new form of "public education" that turns first on results and only second on a place will require a fundamental shift in Americans' thinking. A child will not so much go to *school* as go to *schools,* and these "schools" will take a variety of forms. Some will be designed deliberately to "educate" (schools). Others will exist to entertain, or to sell, or to inform a broad public, not explicitly school-age children. The resulting system will be complex, much more difficult to direct — at least for focused educational purposes — than the existing apparatus. It will almost surely accelerate the trend toward a mix of programs, each competing with others, that in some combination will serve a particular family best (as that family chooses to be served). It will make the often ferocious political battles in some communities over school choice or vouchers seem tame by comparison.

The simple fact is that we have such a system today, whether we like it or not. Existing schools forge ahead largely as they have been traditionally designed to do while the culture around them, from television to hand-held calculators to cheap travel opportunities to the Internet, explodes in thousands of compelling ways. People can argue against Cremin's idea of a configuration of educating institutions, but to assert that they do not exist is to whistle into a hurricane.

The trick will be to use this configuration to preserve the chances of all children, to make sure that none of them is lost, that all of them have a fair and demanding shot at life, that the legitimate needs of families and of the larger communities are well met. This will also require a radical change in thinking among policymakers. It will require a different attitude, especially in the federal government, toward the distribution, direction, and financing of communication. And it will profoundly affect Horace Smith's life — most likely largely for the better. It is easier to teach in a real world than an imaginary one, in a manner and in institutions that capitalize on (or constructively counteract) the ways in which the culture affects adolescents rather than by either ignoring these influences or weakly preaching against them.

This prospect is barely on the education or policy scene yet, save in a number of ambitious individual proposals which are so shocking to the established order that they are marginalized.[9] However, it is increasingly found at the grass-roots level, where more attention is sometimes given to the potential than to the costs of home-based schooling, to the radical expansion of computing, including networking with each student's home, to the use of video of all kinds, and more. As these simple and sensible ideas begin to have a history, they become less shocking and gain recognition within the establishment. The day will soon come when such projects have accreted a mass that will force the next step: a public school that is rooted in a variety of places, from a classroom here and a classroom there to a workplace to the Internet. Ideas and practices now as furtive as they are increasingly ubiquitous will become mainstream, making an end run around the stolid politics of what goes on in school buildings, with all its history and understandable calcification.

In a curious way, perhaps the political estate unwittingly recognizes this possibility. Its lack of interest in serious reform of the schools may come from a deep uncertainty about whether the existing ways of educating really make sense. Cremin — hardly a bomb-throwing pedagogical radical, being an Ivy League professor, a winner of the Bancroft Prize for American History, and the president of Teachers College, Columbia — saw it coming and wished that we would pay attention to it early and well. An America deliberately schooled by configurations of educating institutions rather than by a set of autonomous schoolhouses is not necessarily a weakened America or one inattentive to the common public interest. Indeed, the opposite can be true.

The prospect of fundamental changes in how education is institutionally delivered is as troublesome as it is inevitable. Horace's school will be profoundly affected, one way or another. Pursuing redesign of Franklin High School within its existing walls and customs increasingly unnerves Horace. There is a better way out there, he knows, one that does not build only on the foundations of a particular place, a high school campus.

School reform at the end of this century is cast against a backdrop of extraordinary new influences, both philosophical and practical. Those responsible for the schools cannot pretend that these influences do not exist or are too paltry to deserve attention. On the contrary, they threaten to swamp the public school system as we know it, altering our assumptions about learning and teaching, about what a school in fact is and who has the right to control it. The danger that the educational system may continue to ignore these opportunities depresses Horace. The prospect of facing up to them, of seizing them in the service of substantial reform, however, gives Horace hope.

◆ *The Good New Days*

Getting people to change their minds about what school should be, even in a limited way, is a slow business, one requiring small but persistent steps. One can often see the process in the private sector, where the market is king. What potential parent/tuition payers want is the key. If a school wants to be different, it has to persuade those prospective parents well.

Whitfield School, situated on the line between the city of St. Louis and its western suburbs, looks like many private, independently managed schools serving a public that can largely afford to pay tuition. Its low-slung buildings rest on lots of green grass away from the street. Most are made principally of brick, with white-painted wooden trim. The place exudes an orderly informality, self-confidence, and peace.

Behind all the assurance lies the dragon of often fierce competition. Whitfield survives in a region served by several highly regarded and older private schools and a suburban ring peppered with nationally known public high schools. It is a relatively new school of choice in an area full of highly visible schools, some of which do not cost the families using them any money at all. Whitfield is in what business people call a very tough market.

In 1984, when Mary Burke became principal, Whitfield enrolled thirty-four students. The campus contained three buildings, several in shoddy shape and a few unrefurbished and meant for quite another purpose. A member of the Coalition of Essential Schools since 1986, Whitfield now enrolls 363 students and houses them in one well-organized building — with a science wing, fine arts facilities, and a library as well as the technology to facilitate Internet access from home and school for every student — paid for by $8 million raised in a series of capital fund-raising campaigns. The students, drawn from a wide radius, succeed in the manner of most such independent schools, going off to their chosen colleges. The school has an enviable reputation.

What Burke (backed by the trustees) believed in her first years as principal was that a population existed that both wanted a different kind of secondary school for their children and had enough disposable income to pay for it. Such a view countered the conventional wisdom. Typically, independent schools follow well-established routines: they sell themselves by being what the public believes was there before. Whitfield argued for something that was a bit different — not too different, but different enough to provide schooling that was obviously more relevant to young people than what the competition offered. It decided to offer itself as a substantive choice for all families, particularly those who had previously sought out traditional college preparatory schools but would willingly make the change to a school that was significantly different. At the time, some said that this move was a mistake, that the school would go under. Others, knowing the ferocious energy and pride of Mary Burke and some of her supporters, bet otherwise.

Burke and her predominantly young faculty (the budget did not allow for a stable of veterans) gradually shifted the school's regimen along Essential school lines, with Exhibitions, question-driven assignments, and team teaching. Whitfield made much of these initiatives in public, especially by launching a summer school, jointly operated with the Parkway school district and the University City public schools, which pressed the ideas hard. A six-week course in European history which I visited one summer, for example, was built around court cases, each argued by teams of students. I witnessed the final arguments of the Dreyfus trial, presided over in stern efficiency by a black-robed attorney who was the mother of one of the students. The competition was palpable, the arguments were well researched, and students understood the dilemmas implicit in the case. These kids were engaged in serious ideas in a way that gave those ideas life and with an intensity that assured their retention and their impact.

Conventional wisdom, derived to some extent from polls and focus groups, assumes that the thoughtful public does not want change in its schools as much as order, rigor, and what is in effect predictability. Something new — especially if it requires energy and financial investment — is not in the cards, we are told. Whitfield's experience suggests a different story. In its way, it is kin to Central Park East Secondary School in the public sector, demonstrating that a carefully designed and respectfully argued new kind of school appeals to more than a few families — in Whitfield's case, tuition-paying, largely suburban families, and in CPESS's case, city families, mostly of color.

The case for better schools can be made most effectively by example. The political battles, whether in recalcitrant bureaucracies in the public sector or in the marketplace in the private sector, are fiercer than they should be. Persistent and highly informed leadership is required, as represented by Mary Burke and Deborah Meier. But it can be done. The evidence is clear.

The Whitfield School, St. Louis, Missouri; Mary Burke, head of school. Member of the Coalition of Essential Schools since 1986.

7

Horace's Hope

I RECENTLY shadowed a young man for a day in a well-regarded large suburban secondary school serving a stable, working-class and upper-middle-class, largely white community. His name was Will. I slipped into each of his classes in turn, sitting by prearrangement at the rear of each room, watching and listening.

"Will, do you agree with that?"

The question, about gays and straights, was asked during the second-period health class.

Will pondered. "Umm . . . Well, I guess so."

Though barely six feet tall, Will was the school's basketball star. He went through the day as a member of the second-level academic track, bound, he told me, for a nearby state college: "They've recruited me."

Short-haired and squeaky clean, Will was joined for three of his classes by his girlfriend, a striking junior with long black hair who was the star of the women's basketball team. In the halls during class breaks, they punched each other's arms and giggled.

"Will. Number twenty-three." Now it was algebra, seventh period.

"Umm . . . Twenty-seven . . . the square root of . . . yes, twenty-seven."

The teacher, unsatisfied, moved on. "Patricia?"

Will sat as he always sat in class, almost motionless, feet flat on the floor, unopened books neatly before him. For every class he had a separate notebook, each by this time of year tattered. In no class did he move to write, to gesture, to show any facial expression, to attract any attention. He was like a marble statue of a star athlete frozen in classroom time, an alabaster figure at a schoolboy Hall of Fame.

Will obviously liked that. Those two exchanges in health and algebra — quoted in full — were the only conversations he had in class on any academic issue during the entire seven-period day.

I know from personal experience that it is difficult to capture the interest of a marble icon like Will. His teachers' failure to do so would be okay, they might rationalize, since he would get into state college anyway. Many of them probably were happy to ignore him, as he was so obviously uninterested in what they taught and in them as people. Some surely felt twinges of guilt about this. Should every teacher like and get to know every one of his or her students?

Will did not make any trouble. He was considered a "nice kid." It was unlikely, though, that anyone actually knew what made his mind tick. Cruel stereotypers would say that he did not have a mind, just a jump shot.

Underneath all of this is the astonishing waste — of Will's time, of Will's chances for the future, of his teachers' time, of the community's resources. Will and his pals and his teachers spent the day going through the motions, covering the ground, getting the job done, playing out the routines of school. There was no engagement, no challenge, no insistence that Will (or many of his classmates in several classes; alas, at this school he was not alone) come to some decision or prove something or rise out of his controlled and elaborate lethargy. Indeed, there was no cost for such passivity. Will would make it, by that school's lights. He would do what he was told, and he was rarely told to think hard. If he was learning any habit, it was to keep quiet, to be orderly, to do nothing to attract attention, and to find something outside of class — outside of thinking hard about important things — that was fun and that earned public approbation, such as basketball.

It was Tillson High School all over again, this time in smart suburbia.

School was a warm but vacuous theater, a description that characterizes all too many American high schools, even places that are judged to be good and that students such as Will told me they liked a lot. Almost surely, however, all this inattention was just fine by Will. In other places it is not so appreciated.

In a working-class neighborhood high school I spent a school day shadowing Martha, an impassive but quietly gracious nineteen-year-old. She clearly had a struggle with life. Her father lived in Texas, a thousand miles from this school. Life with her mother was surely unsettling, or so I gleaned from what Martha wanted to tell me. I did not press. She had a heavy relationship (or so her teachers told me) with a man five years her elder.

We marched through the school day, from current events to business mathematics to gym to beginning Spanish to health and more. All the classes were orderly, to a fault: no gum chewing, no talking, sit where I tell you, be quiet. Martha behaved. She was not sullen in her manner, just carefully reserved.

There was no life in the classes, little give-and-take. In Spanish there was sentence drill ("Where is the railroad station?") and a vocabulary game that proceeded up one row and down another. The entire classroom (in which Martha was visibly the oldest student present) slouched, physically and mentally. In current events there was a CNN school service newsclip followed by a lecture by the teacher explaining the most elementary matters ("Ford makes cars outside of America"). In mathematics class mortgage rates were computed, using only rudimentary arithmetic. It was all easy basics, served up as pap.

There was no one event to identify as causing Martha's crisis. The disrespect was a gradual accretion. As we left her sixth-period class, she suddenly hissed intensely in my ear, "I am not stupid, I am not stupid, *I am not stupid.*" It stopped right there. Quickly the mask returned, but her face was flushed. I gave her time to say more. No words came.

This was not only waste. It was cruelty. No teacher or administrator was overtly hurtful. The school's adults simply had no idea what was going on, or if they did (and the mathematics teacher might have had a clue, given the way she once attended to Martha), they found no decisive way to address it. And this was a prize-winning, highly regarded institution, doing all the observable things "well."

Of course there is plenty of overt cruelty affecting adolescents in many communities, especially those containing low-income families. Deborah Meier highlighted this for me with a ghastly, ironic fact. A study of the graduates of the Central Park East elementary schools since their launching (by Meier and her colleagues) in the mid-1970s reported that all those young people, now mostly in their twenties, were still alive.[1] Not one had been struck down on mean streets. That fact had to be one measure of the schools' ability, she felt, to give their children something to live for and the smarts to watch out for themselves — to "cover their backs," as some high school kids have told me. They had hope. Life was not so kind to their peers. That such a fact is notable says worlds, about these schools, about our times, and particularly about us.

I leave schools where I have sensed waste and cruelty and find myself engulfed in the worst kind of self-righteous anger. It is fueled by frustration: I know that most of the adults dealing with the children are good and decent people, largely unappreciated by most other citizens and struggling in extremely difficult circumstances. In my head I therefore rail about the system (whatever it may be) that grandly tolerates routines that force good and decent people into disrespectful and ineffective practice.

My usual ultimate target is the currently popular policy rhetoric about how to improve things by changing the carrots and sticks administered by those at the top of the system and expecting those at the bottom, with meager assistance and with all the existing baggage of regulation and tradition, to reform their ways — or else. At my sourest I compare this with Vietnam War bombing strategies, measured with body counts. When bombing does not appear to win the war, just bomb more. When the test scores do not go up, just give "tougher" tests.

It is an ugly metaphor for the times. I am embarrassed by it, and I struggle to reject it. But it too often comes back after a day of shadowing in weak schools, especially those schools in which the authorities do not acknowledge the weakness. Or it follows a day with administrative and policy people who exhibit little awareness of the facts of being an adolescent and going to school in contemporary America, or after hearing a speech about how we Americans cannot spend any more money or political capital on public education.

It hurts.

And yet Horace Smith, to the surprise of many of his colleagues, is hopeful about the future of American public education. Horace has hope not because he believes that there will be a return to some purported good old days or that the status quo is fine, bedeviled only by a temporary public relations problem. Quite the contrary. And that is what his colleagues who cannot fathom his optimism do not understand.

I have learned to share Horace's hope, whatever the dismay I feel after contemplating the chances in life given to Will and Martha and their kind and however I absorb the sour messages abroad about schools and schooling, about incompetent teachers, rigid bureaucracies, embarrassing test scores, lazy and indulgent students, and high budgets.

Paradoxically, perhaps, all the public controversy itself provides a cause for hope. It is not that all the criticisms are well taken and all those at work in public education deserve the raking-over they are getting. It is, rather, that the invective, whether accurate or far off the mark, has legitimized a searching rethinking of what schooling is all about. What used to be unsayable now is being said — and listened to. No idea is peremptorily dismissed. The taxing ambiguities have brought a freshening of ideas.

For many, this is a frightening moment. It is also a highly promising one. Out of such turbulence can come better schools — or worse, Horace knows, if we blow the opportunity the times are providing us. To my eye, however, some of the trends are very much in the right direction.

Horace Smith is part of a grass-roots movement for reform, one given increasing running room by those very public authorities who are now so assaulted with criticism. It is not without hassle: the lurches of state legislatures, state departments of education, and school boards are a nuisance and often a barrier to the changes Horace wishes to make. Inappropriate regulations, poorly designed but influential assessment systems, and tighter and more paranoid collective bargaining agreements get in the way.

Nonetheless, school-level reform now has visible momentum. This momentum and the increasing public attention that it is receiving are important. As the reform quickens, Horace Smith can take its imperatives as much into account as he takes the dictates from above. Pressure to try new ways to do better has its own authority and public approval and is every bit as powerful as the pressure that says, "Do what you are told and toe the line." Horace is getting into the habit of saying that he won't do as he is told if he is told to do something mindless or ill-advised.

Today there is something for Horace to join, something to make cause with, something that is not wholly a creation of government and the corrosive politics that currently infests so much of it, something that speaks directly to the compromises that so dismay him. It is something more than mere talk, something with an edge, something to do. This something may be an identifiable enterprise, such as the Coalition of Essential Schools, or Dr. James Comer's School Development Project, or E. D. Hirsch's Core Knowledge Foundation, or the Accelerated Schools Project, led by Henry Levin, or Harvard Project Zero. Or, more likely, it may be an informal but sustained gathering of earnest friends or a fresh attitude found in a faculty room or at the meetings of a regional professional group. It gives hope, and the energy to tackle persistent compromises that hope inspires. As a veteran teacher told his younger colleagues at a meeting which I recently attended, "I don't have to apologize anymore." Here and there, more and more, the compromises are being addressed from the grass roots, often in spite of the higher-ups.

Horace knows that the stereotype of the teacher is a crabbed one, and that many in his profession, which is devoted to the task of helping young people learn to use their minds well, have little idea what serious intellectual work in fact involves. They have rarely experienced it themselves, having been through an educational system, including college, that rewarded them for merely showing up and passing through, rather than for presenting serious, rigorous academic work. As a result, coming up with demanding intellectual work for the adolescents they teach is difficult, often poignant labor. It starts with the teachers themselves.

Many critics thus protest. Give authority to these school-level people, with all their well-documented limitations? They will botch it. This, however, is a self-fulfilling prophecy. Tell people of any age that they are not to be trusted, and they will soon believe it and act accordingly. Give a job authority and accountability and able people will flock to it. They will especially gravitate to teaching, with its inherent excitement, variety, and legitimate sense of service — a phenomenon long seen in some private schools and prestigious public magnet schools (not all of which serve only well-scrubbed, academically inclined students) and increasingly seen today.

Horace also appreciates what so many far from the neighborhoods and their schools fail to see: the stubborn quality of decency in so many citizens. There are, as always, the complainers and the people who walk away from their responsibilities for their children. However, too much can be made of them: they are good newspaper copy. Many more people rally around in most communities, especially in an emergency.

Take heart from the school's neighbors? Some will think Horace is blind. The people care? Yes, Horace tells me, the parents and many parents by association (most of us older citizens) do give a damn, and if we see a way to help our public schools, we join in. True, if we are patronized or told that we can briefly "advise" and then "come aboard" when we have had little role in shaping a plan, we tune out. I have experienced happy engagement recently with parents and community members starting a regional public charter school. Meetings of its board of trustees, as provided by the state's legislation for all public schools, are open to all, but the engagement at this school is special. Parents — on the board and in the audience — raise issues, shape the agenda, insistently demand to be consulted, heard, involved, put to work, respected. All feel the power that comes with having chosen this school.

A recent meeting dealt with the "tone of decency" (as the agenda put it) of the school, and it eventually spilled into the collective "tone of decency" of the school's larger community, including what happens at home. (Were rap CDs that are contemptuous of and vicious toward women tolerated at home at the same time that they were banned from school? If so, what does this teach?) This kind of involvement, while it leads to long meetings, will surely serve the children well. Of course, it is possible only in human-scale communities, ones that have real authority over their work. Roaring debates at meetings of school boards representing large constituencies are usually led by factions and special-interest groups. The voice of a parent of a particular youngster with a particular problem is rarely heard, and the energy and commitment of that parent is thus rarely energized.

If people of any age are treated with the dignity they deserve, they respond, in community after community. We see it daily. Often it takes a crisis — a flood on the Mississippi or a bombing on Wall Street or in Oklahoma City — to highlight it. It is patently there. It is a cause for hope.

Doomsayers say that democracy is dying. The number of registered voters who cast ballots drops. The pundits suggest to us, persuasively, that Americans are disgusted with their politicians, that they distrust the system and the government that is its agent. However, being disgusted with the status quo does not mean that we are giving up on democracy. Paradoxically, the opposite is true. So many are unhappy precisely because we believe in the system. We know it can work, and we believe that the alternatives are much worse than the system of government we now have, warts and all.

We complain when we see organized forces outside the democratic system seizing excessive influence. We are sick of being manipulated and lied to ("I merely misspoke . . ."), of being the subjects not of respectful persuasion but of an advertising campaign, of being targets of the same sort of sell that gets us to buy a deodorant or cigarettes. We believe that the American way is better than that and that blatant influence-peddling corrupts what we admire.

People do not want to be patronized and manipulated by their government. They want government to work. They want to admire their government. Is this naive, sentimental patriotism? Not entirely, and there is nothing necessarily wrong with patriotism. We should note the extraordinary surge of interest in local action that followed President Clinton's announcement of Ambassador Walter Annenberg's $500 million personal challenge to the nation for school reform. Annenberg's simple idea — that democracy is at risk of destruction through neglect and violence and that local public schools are the necessary and principal bulwark to resist this decay — struck a powerful chord. Sentimental? Perhaps. Purposeful? Certainly. Realistic? It has to be. What is the alternative, save more decay? People have stepped forward.[2]

There is a host of examples. For instance, I have seen an explosion of energy in parents and local citizens in support of a new district high school in which they will have a respected role and which is designed with their particular children, rather than some stereotype of a child of a certain age (hatched in a remote office building), in mind. A sense of community responsibility is latent in many American neighborhoods, I have found, even those that are racked by poverty and crime or awash in the entitlements of affluence. Too many Americans know that their worlds can be better, that with encouragement those worlds are theirs and they can take charge of them. Give people a cause worth following and the dignity of a necessary role for everyone of every age and they will respond — not quickly or easily, perhaps, but if patiently gathered, they will respond.

I am invited to graduations at Essential schools. Several in communities serving low-income families stick especially in my mind. Most of the young people at these schools have stayed the course, have not dropped out, and have publicly presented their final Exhibitions. Many who never dreamed of going to college are going to college.

Their families know this, and the atmosphere at these gatherings is electric. At one school, student after student gave brief remarks, one coming up after another, spontaneously. Their sustained theme was a poignant and powerful one: "We did what America did not believe we could do." The momentum of this message at this particular gathering — a sad message in its way, as it reminded those assembled that these adolescents knew they were perceived to be people of limited merit — gained force as the long ceremony, some of it colorfully out of control, seemed to burst forth in radiant optimism and determination. Such young people are the fuel of hope. Their schools have made a difference for them, a life-altering difference. Horace has good reason to be hopeful.

The likely shape of a different and useful system of American schools — one created in large part anew — is dimly visible. Key details are still murky and still very much in play, but some outlines are there. The best of these follow.

There will be choice. Every family (not just rich families) will have the ability — indeed, the obligation — to choose among schools for their children. The state will assure that parents do in fact have meaningful choices among schools.

The substance, standard, and culture of each school will be shaped significantly by the families who choose it and the staff who elect to work at it rather than primarily by the deliberations of those families' and the larger communities' elected representatives. Schools will thus differ from one another, often significantly.

Finance will completely or largely be a state (rather than a local) responsibility, and the money will follow the child directly, the full per-pupil allotment going to his or her school. The drift toward state rather than local funding has been under way since the early 1970s. It will continue.

To be a truly public school, worthy of state funding, each school, wherever it is located, will admit every applicant from that state; if there are more applicants than places at the school, it will admit students by lottery. No public policy can more dramatically create the truly common school than this. Civil rights should not and do not need to be weakened by a system of parental choice.

Given general state funding, accountability by and for the schools will be due both to those who chose them — the families, who come first — and to the state. Given the rights of the former, each school should be accountable for the way in which it presents itself and the standard of its work. The state will regularly inspect that school on the basis of the school's own assessment design, objecting only in the most severe cases. The state's essential obligation will be to insist on frequent and public displays by each school of its progress, defined largely by the observable work of its students, which will help provide parents with an accurate picture of the schools. Wise schools will engage outside authorities of their choice to assist in their assessment and public display as they do today with both profit-making and nonprofit agencies, from test publishers to the College Board.

Gradually a spectrum between traditional schooling and formal home schooling will evolve, with what takes place in any one schoolhouse deliberately orchestrated with serious learning activity at home, usually at a computer or book, at a workplace, in an orchestra, as part of a team, as a member of a small neighborhood seminar that is an extension of a larger regional school. "Homework" will change its meaning. Rather than being only studies supplementary to classroom work, it will become activity that is largely independent of the daily, formal school routine, especially for older students. The standard to which the students are held will be met by work at and beyond the formal schoolhouse. The expectation will be that each adolescent will prepare for that standard beyond the immediate shepherding of his teacher in school.

As this configuration of deliberate education emerges, technology — and particularly software — will adapt. Programs will be designed not only to reinforce classroom activity or to entertain in some educational way. They will be freestanding ventures, designed to be used in a variety of ways and organized to prepare a student for an ultimate Exhibition.

In this way students will go to multiple schools, places that in planned combination provide for formal education. For most contemporary adolescents, this will at first appear to call for just a modest change in behavior, as their learning is now influenced powerfully by multiple sources of information. What will be starkly new for them, however, is finding that these sources can and must be taken seriously. Educators, parents, and the media and publishing industries will have to create incentives for students to use all of these sources resolutely — no mean feat. But it will happen, because that is the way the culture increasingly educates itself and because configurations make as much financial as educational sense. Better yet is the fact that these "beyond the schoolhouse" opportunities can at one leap transcend the boundaries of geography and thus of class, ethnicity, and race.

As a practical matter, *systems of schools will emerge,* each representing a particular educational style or opportunity and each governing itself within state authority. For example, one set of schools might emphasize a particular teaching approach, such as that arising from the work of Maria Montessori or from E. D. Hirsch's Core Knowledge

Foundation or from the Coalition of Essential Schools. Another might involve a substantial system of computer-driven connected instruction. Others might emphasize, for adolescents, substantial time and formal learning in a workplace other than a traditional school building. The momentum of tradition and expected practice will, at least for a generation, hold these approaches to substantial common ground, as they do today. The temptation of central authorities to micro-manage them, however, will have to be stoutly resisted. These systems of schools would overlap. The options available to families would appear much like those now represented by higher education.[3]

Choice. Variety. Truly open schools. Equitable finance. Power deliberately tilted toward the families of the children served and the professionals who teach them. The deliberate use of various orchestrated configurations of learning, not just the schoolhouse. All of these issues are more or less on the political table today. Over the past decade, interest in them has picked up substantial momentum.

These ideas are consistent with the drift of contemporary public sentiment as expressed in policy or, implicitly, by what is happening in practice. They reflect the prevalent view that centralized government is an inept and inappropriate tool to set and shape the substance and standards of school policy and practice. They reflect the view that disproportional authority for these purposes should be given to the families affected and the professionals to whom those families entrust their children. Centralized government is needed as a financier (that is, the dispenser of the people's money), as a documenter, persuader, supporter, advocate for neglected children, truth-teller, but not, except at the extremes, a director.

These ideas reflect the belief that a market — involving competition and real choice among schools — is a better, if not complete or perfect, regulator of schooling than the traditional educational and political authorities and their expert allies in the teaching profession.

They reflect a prominent view loudly expressed today in the context of the debate over national health care: I wish to choose my own doctor rather than be assigned one by the state. In like manner, I wish to pick my children's school rather than have the state do the choosing.

These ideas address reality, however painful or inconvenient that reality is. They are attuned to the extraordinary variety of communities and interests in this country, a variety that is ill served by centralized control, which usually demands standardization. What works well for a small town in northeastern Arizona might be inappropriate for a precinct in Pittsburgh. These ideas recognize and dignify our diversity.

They provide an end run around the *Milliken* decision of the United States Supreme Court, which ruled that the suburbs (usually wealthy and white) have no constitutional responsibility to join in racial integration with the school systems in the central cities (usually poor and disproportionately nonwhite).[4] If the money follows the child and if that child's family can enter him or her in its school of choice, *wherever that may be* — a school that must admit all applicants, using a lottery system if necessary, in order to receive public funding — the opportunity for more class and racial integration, where it is desired, can proceed. Currently it cannot proceed at all, at least for the poor, even if some families — poor and rich — wish that it could. Geographical boundaries, mostly reflecting the demographic and political priorities of the past, dictate current school policy. These boundaries will be pierced.

These ideas address the fact that there are deep and understandable disagreements not only among citizens but among experts on just what an excellent education might be and how we would know it when we saw it. In the emerging public school system, no one point of view dominates; the market of ideas allows both variety and contention among serious positions. This will be untidy, and those who believe that there is a virtue in cultural orderliness will no doubt be unhappy. Unfortunately, our world is untidy, free minds are untidy, and to be genuine and useful, our institutions must reflect that rather than present a spurious uniformity.

They address the compromises that so trouble Horace Smith, by providing channels and incentives for the creation of new schools or the redesign of existing schools that follow more sensible regimens than those now widely in use and largely cemented in place by regulatory practice. This encourages Horace, keeps him at his work, and attracts imaginative and talented people into the school business.

These ideas carry with them important side effects. They imply that school leaders must become more entrepreneurial than exclusively managerial, becoming leaders of schools that have a distinct character rather than agents of someone else's idea of what a school ought to be.

They put an extraordinary responsibility on the profession and the academic community at large to seek out and place before the public evidence of what is working in schools, by a variety of definitions, and what is not, and to define what kinds of investment different goals require, thus pushing into visibility the weaknesses and strengths of the diverse schools that citizens are choosing among. The watchdogs have to be the people themselves, not central governments (except at the extremes, such as when a school gives evidence of appalling neglect or has doctored evidence about its graduates' performance).

These ideas will challenge, directly or by circumvention, the elaborate thickets of educational regulation, certification, and accreditation, which more often than not reflect the vagaries of past academic politics and distrust of local authorities rather than considered and proven practices. They depend on persuasion rather than coercive control.

These systems will be messy, both in their diversity and in the confrontations that will result from their competition. Many will find this aggravating, undercutting the (spurious) spirit of togetherness expressed by main-line education groups.

But these ideas force a test of the proposition that healthy democracy depends on an ultimate trust in and of the people, no matter how small the unit in which the people are gathered for a particular purpose is. Either we trust the people or we don't.

These ideas challenge the notion that the primary purpose of the public schools is to teach a common culture, an American way, American ideals. Diversity is centrifugal, some will argue; the common school is the only way to give coherence to what it is to be an American. However, the reality is that we have in the media the most powerful common carrier of mass culture in history. It is so powerful that its existence changes the necessary role for schools from creators of the culture to respectful critics of that culture.

In this regard, the federal government has new and heavy responsibilities. The mass media must be seen as a fundamental piece of public education, a full participant with the schools. Federal responsibility might play out in a number of ways. The financing of useful programming and the maintenance of independent channels devoted to educational purposes is a clear governmental responsibility. Free access by all citizens to the artistic and intellectual treasures of the society must become an absolute right, like free public education itself. The electronic library is the lineal descendant of the public library and is crucial for the support of an intelligent people. Its costs should be wholly met by a tax on those making commercial use of the common good represented by the broadcast channels. There is growing public sentiment for these ideas, only just now powerful enough to affect federal policy.

The outlines of a new kind of public education, then, are visible. One danger is that government will adopt the easy parts and ignore the difficult ones, such as providing fair compensatory funding or access to technology for each poor or handicapped child, or providing access to any publicly financed school in the state, not only those within a historically established district. Another is that the leap from dependence on a rule-driven hierarchical system to trust of families is more than the political system can tolerate and the temptation on the part of the state to keep control will be too strong. Loosening control is always more difficult than tightening it. A third is the danger that removing education from the administrative status it now enjoys within government, weak though that is, will lessen leaders' interest in keeping an eye on the educational needs of its citizens.

All these concerns are real ones. Are they greater than those implicit in going along with the present system? We must always measure the risks of the new against those of the old. The reality is that the currents toward a new sort of American educational system are already flowing. There can be no turning back. The trick will be to understand those new currents and to ride, and thus direct, the best of them.

The traditional American system of schools was in large measure designed exactly a century ago. It has served us well, but times and conditions change. America in 1995 is not the America of 1895. Not surprisingly, a new system of schools is emerging, one that is more complex and potentially more powerful than the one we inherited. If wisely and resolutely shaped, such a system can serve the people and democracy well. Such is a source of Horace's hope.

My wife, Nancy, and I called at the office of the principal of a large city high school in the Southwest and found her coming out of her conference room with a mother and her daughter. Mother seemed weak, painfully shy, withdrawn. Daughter, probably sixteen or seventeen years old, was quiet but talked easily with the principal, Angelica Morales. Angelica showed them out before turning to us, with a final word to the daughter suggesting that "we should try this."

As we started on our ritual principal's office coffee, Angelica explained about this pair. Both had recently arrived from Mexico; they had only each other for support. The mother was sickly, unable to work, unskilled in English, frightened and disoriented by her new American surroundings. The daughter, Maria, was the family's sole source of income, in effect the head of the household. She worked every weekday afternoon immediately after school and into evening, up to shortly after midnight, as a cashier and usher at a movie theater. On Saturdays and Sundays the duties went from shortly after noon to midnight again. School and homework were tucked in around these obligations.

The problem at school was not Maria's performance. She was passing all of her courses. The issue was that she was habitually late in the morning and that she often fell asleep in class. For obvious reasons, this annoyed her teachers. Although some probably sympathized with Maria's situation, tolerating persistent early-in-the-day class-cutting set a bad example. And having a student sleep soundly in class does dull one's teaching style (to put it charitably). The teachers complained, out of concern for Maria as much as for the integrity of their classes.

We never learned just what Angelica did in this situation. Clearly some sort of accommodation was afoot — part-time enrollment, perhaps. Maria's situation, though, was transparent. Here was a teenager taking charge not only of her life but of her mother's. She was a young person of substantial fiber. She juggled two full-time lives and more, with gritty determination, but she could not always hide her exhaustion. Angelica's school would bend for her, we knew, in some sensible way. Maria would make it because she was already an adult, in the best sense.

There are many teenagers who are not like Maria, who mindlessly wander around the malls, live shamelessly off other people, and sleep their hangovers off in class. We hear endlessly about them. A branch of the film industry depends on them as the lead characters in teen movies. However, there are many Marias, and more can be recruited.

Serious secondary education requires the commitment of its students. They have to work hard; they are not merely genial empty vessels waiting to be filled with knowledge. They need the commitment and determination of Maria. But the schools for them have to be committed and determined too. The temptation to pass the buck is almost irresistible. Look at Maria, people will say, she did it by pulling herself up by her bootstraps and not by depending on us. All other kids must do that too, and we adults can both back away from our responsibilities and feel smug about that withdrawal.

In this, one of the richest of all societies, Maria and her mother should not have to live on the precarious margin of survival. Further, for our collective benefit, Maria's obvious talents should be protected, nurtured, propelled. To allow her merely to pass her courses, to conspire with her to give little attention to homework, sells her terribly short. This is very likely a powerful young woman, one who could give a great deal to society. Society's neglect of her is costly, in every respect.

Public education is an idea, not a structure. The idea is that every citizen must have access to the culture and to the means of enriching that culture. It arises from the belief that we are all equal as citizens, and that we all thereby have rights and obligations to serve the community as well as ourselves. To meet those obligations, we must use our informed intelligence. Schools for all assure the intelligence of the people, the necessary equipment of a healthy democracy. A wise democracy invests in that equipment.

Public education, then, is not at all or necessarily the same thing as our current system of schools. Other means to give the people access and intelligence — new configurations of educating institutions — may be better, more appropriate to our time, more respectful of current exigencies. If we are wise, we will consider them, however much they may challenge the conventional ways of doing things.

To the extent that we embrace that challenge and the fundamental American philosophy behind it — that a free and powerful education is the absolute right of every citizen and that this education must be first and foremost seen as the mainspring of a democratic community — we can be hopeful.

For Horace Smith, the hope is also more personal, arising from the particular adolescents all around him — their color and brashness, their gawkiness, their risk-taking, their naiveté about the world, which sucks so many of them into optimism, however unrealistic. The high theater of the school hallway never ceases to amuse him, and the diversions of the kids' little passions tickle his love of fiction, creating tiny comic stories in his head. The dance of youth is timeless and beautiful in its awkwardness.

Most of the young people are resilient in the face of either the lures of affluence or the savagery of neglect. Horace worries more about them than they do about themselves, and he is ashamed when it dawns on his students how little American culture actually values them. Most of the kids, however, sweep this away, not so much with anger as with tacit rejection. *To hell with you, old-timer. We'll go it on our own, and we'll make it.*

Horace knows that some will and many won't. But the energy is there, fueled as much by inexperience as by grit. With all its unreality, it yet insistently radiates the strength and inventiveness of humankind. In dark days, such light brings hope.

APPENDIXES

ACKNOWLEDGMENTS

NOTES

Appendix A

The Coalition of Essential Schools

Horace's Hope is the third volume in a story about American secondary education.

The impetus for all this writing began for me twenty years ago, during my nine years of service as a teacher and headmaster at Phillips Academy, in Andover, Massachusetts. Phillips, a powerful if not perfect academic boarding school, approached some things differently from its more traditional day-school cousins, most of them public high schools. However, most of its regimen, like that of the public schools, was remarkably similar to the routines of secondary schooling seen in this country since the late 1800s.

In the early 1960s I had published a book on Charles William Eliot and the 1893 Committee of Ten on Secondary School Studies, which he chaired (*Secondary Schools at the Turn of the Century,* New Haven: Yale University Press, 1964), and I had thus immersed myself in the issues of turn-of-the-century adolescents and their schooling. Eighty years after the publication of the report of Eliot's Committee of Ten, I was struck by how powerfully present not only its basic ideas but many of the specific practices for the sort of schooling it promulgated still were.

The report's main-line subjects — mathematics, English, science, history, and foreign language — became and remain to this day the core of the traditional academic regimen. (It was not so in Eliot's time. The promotion of science, at the expense of the classical languages, was bitterly fought during the late 1890s. In some quarters, chemistry, physics, and biology were felt to lack general "disciplinary value.") Eliot's reduction of the curriculum to detailed charts of times and sequences, which were to be universal across all secondary schools, was unusual in its day. The practice now is deeply embedded. The belief that preparation for college was no more or less than a preparation for life annoyed many. The majority of educators today accept that judgment.

There is nothing at all wrong with tradition and cleaving tightly to that which works well. But it is an error to continue what later times have discovered to be wrong-headed.

The more I listened to my public and private school colleagues during the 1970s, the more I came to believe that while what we were doing in our schools was generous and well intentioned, the design of the work often defied common sense when scrutinized carefully. Teach mathematics and physics or literature and visual art as utterly separate entities? Break the day into little fifty-minute globules of time and expect thoughtful work? Assign lots of writing but never allow teachers the time to read and critique it? Treat every child of the same age in essentially the same way?

Too much made too little sense. With the encouragement of several Phillips Academy trustees, I determined to find out more, to try to watch and to listen in a wide variety of schools, thereby to understand better what it was to grow up adolescent and go to school in America in our own time. Generous foundations stepped forward to support this work, and I resigned from Andover in 1981 in order to pursue it with a number of colleagues. We called our collective effort A Study of High Schools.

We on the study watched and listened and documented and read and argued and ultimately wrote. Arthur G. Powell, Eleanor Farrar, and David K. Cohen published *The Shopping Mall High School* (Boston: Houghton Mifflin, 1985), a description and telling critique arising from the systematic observation of fifteen secondary schools across the country. Robert M. Hampel issued *The Last Little Citadel* (Boston: Houghton Mifflin, 1986), a history of American secondary education since 1940, decades of extraordinary growth for the public high schools.

My task was to produce a more general and "popular" volume — *Horace's Compromise* (Boston: Houghton Mifflin, 1984), which was my critique of secondary schools as we currently run them. Once the book had been published, foundations again stepped forward and urged me to transcend that critique, to try to ascertain what positive things might be said about serious schooling and to find some schools around the country that wanted to apply these better ideas to their everyday practice. I was afforded the chance to move to Brown University, in Providence, Rhode Island, both to teach and to base my new activist work there. I moved the nascent project to Brown in 1984 and with a small group of colleagues started what we called the Coalition of Essential Schools.

Why "essential"? We had a double meaning in mind: essential in that the work we envisioned was tellingly needed, and essential in that the schools choosing to be involved would focus on the intellectual core of schooling, at the expense of "extras," which appeared to them and us to be weakening the ultimate work of the students.

A first description of the Coalition's effort appeared as an appendix to the second edition of *Horace's Compromise,* issued in 1988. We had designed the Coalition's work to be carefully respectful of the particular place and time in which each school found itself. Our view was that excellence and vitality in schools arises from the particular people within them and the community in which that school resides. Accordingly, we prescribed no "model" to "implement." We came with no panacea. We believed that each community had to find its own way. However, what we accepted in common was a set of ideas, ones that appeared to us to invest every good school we knew.

When I drafted this list of ideas, I was determined to keep it short, to focus on a few key elements. What are now called the common principles of the Coalition of Essential Schools were not meant to be exhaustive, and in their generality were meant as much to provoke thought and imagination as to give specific guidance.

The list as I prepared it in 1983, which continues to serve the Coalition, is as follows:

1. The school should focus on helping adolescents learn to use their minds well. Schools should not be "comprehensive" if such a claim is made at the expense of the school's intellectual purpose.

2. The school's goals should be simple: that each student master a limited number of essential skills and areas of knowledge. While these skills and areas will, to varying degrees, reflect the traditional academic disciplines, the program's design should be shaped by the intellectual and imaginative powers and competencies that students need rather than necessarily by "subjects" as conventionally defined. The aphorism "less is more" should dominate: curricular decisions should be guided by the aim of thorough student mastery and achievement rather than by an effort merely to cover content.

3. The school's goals should apply to all students, while the means to these goals will vary as those students themselves vary. School practice should be tailor-made to meet the needs of every group or class of adolescents.

4. Teaching and learning should be personalized to the maximum feasible extent. Efforts should be directed toward a goal that no teacher have direct responsibility for more than eighty students. To capitalize on this personalization, decisions about the details of the course of study, the use of students' and teachers' time, and the choice of teaching materials and specific pedagogies must be unreservedly placed in the hands of the principal and staff.

5. The governing practical metaphor of the school should be student-as-worker rather than the more familiar metaphor of teacher-as-deliverer-of-instructional-services. Accordingly, a prominent pedagogy will be coaching, to provoke students to learn how to learn and thus to teach themselves.

6. Students entering secondary school studies are those who can show competence in language and elementary mathematics. Students of traditional high school age but not yet at appropriate levels of competence to enter secondary school studies will be provided intensive remedial work to assist them quickly to meet these standards. The diploma should be awarded upon a successful final demonstration of mastery for graduation — an "Exhibition." This Exhibition by the student of his or her grasp of the central skills and knowledge of

the school's program may be jointly administered by the faculty and by higher authorities. As the diploma is awarded when earned, the school's program proceeds with no strict age grading and with no system of "credits earned" by "time spent" in class. The emphasis is on the students' demonstration that they can do important things.

7. The tone of the school should explicitly and self-consciously stress values of unanxious expectation ("I won't threaten you but I expect much of you"), of trust (until abused), and of decency (the values of fairness, generosity, and tolerance). Incentives appropriate to the school's particular students and teachers should be emphasized, and parents should be treated as essential collaborators.

8. The principal and teachers should perceive themselves as generalists first (teachers and scholars in general education) and specialists second (experts in one particular discipline). Staff should expect multiple obligations (teacher-counselor-manager) and a sense of commitment to the entire school.

9. Ultimate administrative and budget targets should include, in addition to total student loads per teacher of eighty or fewer pupils, substantial time for collective planning by teachers, competitive salaries for staff, and an ultimate per-pupil cost not to exceed that at traditional schools by more than 10 percent. To accomplish this, administrative plans may have to show the phased reduction or elimination of some services now provided students in many traditional comprehensive secondary schools.

At the time, none of these principles struck me as radical or fantastic. Only two were fundamentally ideological — that the purpose of schooling was intellectual, the resourceful use by the young person of his or her mind; and that this goal should apply to all young citizens without exception. However, these goals had deep roots in American democratic tradition.

Two of the principles had some deliberate specificity, in each case to make a point. First, teachers' total student loads (that is, the total number of students in their several classes) were not to exceed eighty, a number far smaller than that found in most American secondary schools, except those serving the affluent. Our research persuaded us that if a teacher could not get to know his or her students well, a great deal of consequence was lost. The typical high school load of 120 to 175 students — the root of most of Horace's painful compromises — made much of what was essential impossible, at least for all but a small group of favored or highly motivated students. (Ten years later, many in Essential schools say that eighty is itself too many, that fewer than fifty is necessary — and they have crafted such loads in schools within typical per-pupil expenditures.)

Second, schools had to work their reform within existing budgets — the assumption being not that more money might not be nice or even needed, but that it was unlikely to be forthcoming. Serious reform assumes certain facts, and one of the most vexing is finance. While more moneys are legitimately needed in most places, to hold off reform while waiting for gargantuan budget increases is to wait forever in the current political and economic climate. The addition of 10 percent, mentioned in the common principles, was from the start pressed on me by colleagues who argued that no liberal advocate for schools should ever appear to accept a budget status quo. I gave in a bit too quickly to that political logic. More seriously, I failed to calculate the up-front costs of reform — the planning and retraining and politicking required to turn each school. While these are to some extent one-time expenditures, they are not inconsequential, and the willingness of governing authorities to order reform and then to provide few resources for its accomplishment has been all too evident in recent years, with predictably limited results.

The rest of the ideas were, it seemed to me, common sense, even if — when taken with the seriousness they deserved — they implied substantial changes in the way that most high schools currently functioned.

My colleagues in Essential schools resolutely involved themselves with these ideas and have added to our store of understanding of what might or might not work in secondary schools. From time to time some of them have suggested a tenth principle. The two most commonly mentioned are one calling for democratic school governance and one for a dictum regarding appropriate respect and authority for students. The most neatly focused yet, in the form of an aphorism, came recently from a student in an Essential school in England: "It is cool to be clever."

From the Coalition's earliest days, I was repeatedly asked what specifically was meant by these ideas and how they might play out in combination. Accordingly, in 1992 I published a new volume, *Horace's School* (Boston: Houghton Mifflin), which gave a detailed example of how one "remedy" might work, reflecting Essential school ideas. Much of this was gratefully gleaned from the ongoing work of my colleagues in Essential schools.

By the early 1990s a number of elementary schools approached us, telling us that strong primary school practice has long reflected CES ideas and that they wished to join our conversation. Deborah Meier and I adjusted the existing common principles modestly to the realities of schools serving younger children, and a unit organized and led by elementary school colleagues was established at the Center for Collaborative Education in New York City. As our collective work has developed, we have learned that a pathway of coherent and consistent schooling from the earliest grades to high school graduation makes extraordinarily good sense and that this is possible administratively in some school districts (and is de rigueur in many private schools and small, usually rural, public school districts).

By early 1996, the Coalition had grown to more than a thousand schools at one stage of work or another, each striving to fashion its own appropriate design that reflected the Coalition's simple, basic ideas. Some 250 were beyond the exploring and planning stages and were fully engaged in their work with children. The overall effort has, however, barely begun. Serious change is slow business, and a well-studied judgment about the practicality of Essential school ideas, if they have been taken seriously, will have to emerge gradually.

The Coalition's common principles as cast for elementary school practice follow:

1. The school should focus on helping young people develop the habit of using their minds well. Schools should not attempt to be compre-

hensive if such a claim is made at the expense of the school's central intellectual purpose. Schools should be learner-centered, addressing students' social and emotional development as well as their academic progress.

2. The school's academic goal should be simple: that each student master a limited number of essential skills and areas of knowledge. The aphorism "less is more" should dominate. Curricular decisions should be guided by student interest, developmentally appropriate practice, and the aim of thorough student mastery and achievement. Students of all ages should have many opportunities to discover and construct meaning from their own experiences.

3. The school's goals should apply to all students, while the means to these goals will vary as those students themselves vary. Teachers who know their students well can individualize instruction without limiting their expectations of any students. Strong habits of mind are necessary for all.

4. Teaching and learning should be personalized to the maximum extent feasible. To capitalize on this personalization, decisions about the details of the course of study, the use of students' and teachers' time, and the choice of teaching materials and specific pedagogies must be unreservedly placed in the hands of the principal and staff.

5. The governing practical metaphor of the school should be student-as-worker rather than the more familiar metaphor of teacher-as-deliverer-of-instructional-services. Accordingly, a prominent pedagogy will be coaching and guiding, to enable students to understand how they learn and thus to teach themselves and each other as members of a community of learners.

6. Teaching and learning should be documented and assessed with tools based on student performance of real tasks. Multiple forms of evidence, ranging from ongoing observation of the learner to completion of specific projects, should be used to better understand the learner's strengths and needs and to plan for further assistance. Students should have opportunities to exhibit their expertise before family and community. The final diploma should be awarded upon a successful demonstration of mastery of gradation — an "Exhibition." As the diploma is awarded when earned, the school's program

proceeds with no strict age grading and with no system of "credits earned" by "time spent" in class. The emphasis is on the students' demonstration that they can do important things.

7. Families should be vital members of the school community. Close collaboration between home and school yields respect and understanding. Correspondingly, the tone of the school should explicitly and self-consciously stress values of unanxious expectation ("I won't threaten you and I expect much of you"), of trust (until abused), and of decency (the values of fairness, generosity, and tolerance).

8. The principal and teachers should perceive themselves as generalists first (teachers and scholars in general education) and specialists second (experts in one particular discipline). Staff should expect multiple obligations (teacher-counselor-manager) and a sense of commitment to the entire school.

9. Ultimate administrative and budget targets should include substantial time for collective planning by teachers, competitive salaries for staff, and an ultimate per-pupil cost not to exceed that at traditional schools by more than 10 percent. To accomplish this, administrative plans may have to show the phased reduction or elimination of some services now provided students in many traditional schools.

Appendix B

The Coalition of Essential Schools: A National Research Context

Margaret M. MacMullen

Over the past decade many members of the Coalition of Essential Schools have participated in a rich and growing body of regional and national research projects. Conducted by universities and private research organizations, these projects describe the nature and document the effects of school restructuring. Many of the studies follow schools over a period of several years; some take advantage of the huge databases that track a given national sample of students over time; and all have developed promising methods for investigating this ambitious and complex reform effort.

Since the reform effort is young, most studies have focused on implementation issues and the effects of Coalition-like restructuring on school life. This research has helped to clarify the goals of restructuring, reveal the complex and often puzzling nature of implementation, and identify promising strategies. But increasingly, studies are tackling the thorny problem of the effect of reforms on student performance. Three major research efforts either are complete or have released preliminary data on student achievement; a fourth effort has produced case studies of a number of schools that, taken together, offer insights into student progress. All four include Coalition schools in their study samples.

The results are extremely encouraging. When the changes embodied in the Coalition's nine common principles are fully implemented both inside the classroom and in the school as a whole, the effects are consistent, beneficial, and significant. Such schools have increased student engagement in academic work and raised student achievement and parent, teacher, and student satisfaction; they have had a positive effect on student behavior and promoted equity in achievement among different groups of students. In addition, several studies identify which changes have the most impact and show how best to support the changes. A clear and strong finding across studies is that the more fully the changes are implemented, the more powerful their effect is.

The First Study

In 1993, the results of a pioneering study on the question of restructuring effects on student achievement were published. This report, while somewhat limited by its size and geographic focus, was the first to identify the positive relationship between schools' commitment to restructuring and outcomes for students that has been confirmed in later studies.

Over a three-year period, 1988 to 1991, Regina Kyle (1993) assessed the long-term joint effort by the Jefferson County, Kentucky, schools and the Gheens Professional Academy to effect significant reform in their 131 schools. Kyle and the Gheens Foundation, which had provided substantial support for restructuring schools, wanted to know whether the changes had made a difference for students.

Since involvement in the reform effort was voluntary, the amount of restructuring in district schools by 1988 ranged from none to intensive and sustained. Three categories of schools emerged. Group I schools had made a sustained commitment to restructuring, and their reforms could be considered systemic. Group II schools were in the exploration stages, trying out a variety of reforms without having developed a clear focus. Group III schools had not yet attempted any reforms. The Group I category was narrowed to include schools with at least a three- to five-year history of systemic approaches; then schools in

Groups II and III were selected to match Group I on demographic characteristics.

Kyle then developed three measures of effectiveness. The positive involvement indicator included attendance, suspensions, dropouts, graduation rates, and parent and student satisfaction. The basic improvement indicator measured improvement in scores from CTBS standardized tests administered to students by the system each year. The average annual improvement rate indicator showed the progress in CTBS scores between 1988 and 1991.

She found that across all levels — elementary, middle, and high school — Group I outperformed both Groups II and III on all three indicators. For example, at the high school level on the basic improvement indicator, Group I increased the percentages of students at or above the fiftieth percentile 83 percent of the time. Groups II and III increased the percentages 67 percent of the time. In average annual improvement, Group I improved at an average rate of 6.8 percent per year, with Groups II and III improving 4.5 percent and 4.6 percent, respectively. The positive involvement indicator found Group I improving 85 percent of the time, with Groups II and III improving 50 percent and 65 percent, respectively. Since the Group I high schools included a number of Coalition schools, these findings are especially relevant and encouraging.

Asking Two Important Questions

The Center on Organization and Restructuring of Schools at the University of Wisconsin is nearing the end of an ambitious five-year effort to investigate the effects of restructuring on student learning. The center has sponsored several sets of studies, of which two are of special interest to the Coalition. One set is on a large scale and asks whether school restructuring increases student achievement. The second set narrows the focus to twenty-four restructuring schools to examine whether they promote intellectual rigor and if so, how. Since these studies have different emphases and approaches, it is instructive to view them separately before exploring how they fit together.

A Large-Scale View of Restructuring and Student Achievement

Valerie Lee and Julia Smith conducted the first large-scale national studies of the effects of high school restructuring on achievement. In 1994 they looked at the effects of restructuring from eighth to tenth grade on a large sample of tenth-grade students. In a study recently released, they examined the achievement of the same students in twelfth grade. In addition, in the second study they were able to identify specific areas of school organization that had the greatest impact on student learning. In both studies they characterized restructuring as the movement away from a bureaucratic or more traditional form of organization to a more communal one.

These two organizational definitions were introduced and tested in earlier work (Bryk and Driscoll, 1988; Lee, Smith, and Bryk, 1993). A bureaucratically organized high school is marked by its high degree of specialization and, frequently, its large size. Teachers work in separate departments or programs, with little collaboration; students choose from multiple and varied course offerings; and management and decision-making are handled in a top-down style. In contrast, a communally organized high school is characterized by more personal contact and, frequently, by smaller size. Roles and tasks are more flexible, and teachers work together toward a common set of goals and share in decision-making. Students share a common curriculum. The large comprehensive high school, in favor since Conant's advocacy in the late fifties, is an example of the bureaucratically organized school. Coalition schools strive toward a more communal structure.

Lee and Smith set out to determine whether schools incorporating elements of restructuring that move them toward a more communal organization have a positive effect on student achievement. Using available data, they were able to show beneficial effects on both achievement and equity through the tenth grade. They then designed their second study to see if those effects were sustained throughout high school and to determine with more precision which aspects of organizational change were most powerful. For their database in both studies they used the three rounds of the National Educational Longitudinal Study of 1988 (NELS), which tracks the educational progress of a large national sample of students and schools. By screening the data for their specific needs — including a minimum of five NELS students in each school site — they ended up with a sample of 11,794 sophomores in 820 high schools, averaging 14 students per school, for their first study and 9,570 seniors in 789 high schools, averaging 12 students per school, in their second study.

The first study. From a NELS school questionnaire completed by principals, Lee and Smith selected thirty practices commonly regarded as school reforms. The practices ranged from reforms that support the bureaucratic structure to those that move schools toward a communal organization. Since Lee and Smith had hypothesized that reform practices compatible with their definition of communal schools would be the least common reforms in schools, they needed to determine how often the thirty reforms occurred. To this end, using the questionnaire responses, they calculated the probability that each practice would be present in their sample of schools. They then ranked the reforms by likelihood of their presence.

As they had hypothesized, the reform practices least likely to be in use were those that departed most from conventional practice and promoted a more communal school structure; they called this cluster of practices the restructuring group. Two other categories, moderate and traditional, emerged. Both groups of reforms adhered more closely to a bureaucratic model.

The sample schools were then classified into groups. "Traditionally reformed schools" engaged in one or more moderate or traditional reforms but fewer than three restructuring reforms. Schools were considered "restructured" if they practiced at least three of the restructuring reforms on the list.

Lee and Smith then looked at how student achievement in mathematics, science, history, and reading compared among the groups. They reported that "the results of the study were clear and consistent: Schools that implemented three or more restructuring practices posted significantly higher academic achievement than other schools. Those gains were more equitably distributed among students from different socioeconomic backgrounds. Schools with more traditional reforms in place outperformed schools with no reform practices at all, but didn't perform as well as schools undertaking reforms consistent with restructuring" (Lee, Smith, and Croninger, 1995a, p. 5).

This is very good news for Coalition schools. The restructuring practices that produce a communal organization are consistent with those implemented by Coalition schools. In addition, given the Coalition's support for small learning environments, it can take encouragement from one of the study's strongest findings: that students do better in smaller schools (Lee and Smith, 1994b).

The second study. For this investigation Lee and Smith (joined by R. G. Croninger) used the same sample of students, now in twelfth grade, the same definitions for restructuring schools and traditionally reformed schools, and essentially the same methodology, but this time they focused on achievement in mathematics and science. Their first goal was to ascertain whether the positive effects on achievement and equity in the early years of high school continued through twelfth grade. And their news was good. They discovered that gains in achievement in the two subjects continued over the last two years of high school. The gains were less dramatic but still significant. And the gap between students from lower and higher socioeconomic groups remained narrower.

The authors report further: "Rather than shrinking or dying away after the first two years of high school, when we might expect students to be most influenced by schools that are relatively new to them, these effects endure over the entire course of high school — continuing to influence how much students learn and who is learning. In fact, the organizational and restructuring effects actually increase somewhat in the latter years of high school" (Lee, Smith, and Croninger, 1995b, p. 27).

The greatest contribution of this study, however, lies in the results of its second research goal: to identify which organizational characteristics of high school promote these significant effects on student learning. The first study was able to identify a broad category of restructuring practices that affected student achievement and seemed to move a school away from bureaucracies toward communities. But the second study was able to determine that only a small set of school features actually accounted for the differences in learning related to restructuring.

The four features the researchers isolated were classroom teaching that fosters active learning and student's construction as well as reproduction of knowledge; a narrow curriculum which offers little variability in academic courses; teachers who together take a high level of responsibility for student learning; and steady pressure on students to pursue academic excellence. They named these features respectively authentic instruction, common curriculum, collective responsibility, and academic press. The study revealed that between grades eight to ten and ten to twelve, students in schools scoring high on the four indicators would have the following achievement gains in mathematics and science over students in schools scoring low:

- authentic instruction — from about 50 to 100 percent higher
- common curriculum — from 46 to 100 percent higher
- collective responsibility — from 54 percent to 137 percent higher
- academic press — from 38 percent to 60 percent higher (Newmann and Wehlage, pp. 25, 37).

Taken together, these studies offer strong, convincing evidence for the direction recommended by the Coalition's nine common principles. They lend unequivocal support to the belief that intellectual excellence should be the goal for all students, they support one important aspect of the principle "less is more," and they assert the importance of a school community that knows all students well. Lee, Smith, and Croninger argue that "these studies provide solid support for a body of sociological research that school organization matters, and that the optimal organizational form for high schools is more communal than bureaucratic" (1995b, p. 30).

A More Intensive View

By taking a close look at a smaller number of restructuring schools, a second set of studies sponsored by the Wisconsin Center on Organization and Restructuring of Schools was able to corroborate and elaborate on the Lee and Smith findings. The School Restructuring Study, completed in 1995 (Newmann, Marks, and Gamoran, in press), was an intensive study of twenty-four substantially restructuring schools — eight each at elementary, middle, and high school levels. Through a national search, schools that had changed their organizational features substantially from those of more traditional schools were selected. Almost 140 teachers and more than 3000 students in schools from 16 states and 22 districts participated in the study. Although not named in the study, nine of the twenty-four schools were Coalition schools, making the findings especially germane. Through classroom observations, site visits, extensive interviews and surveys, and scoring of more than 3000 pieces of student work, Fred Newmann, the center's director, and his colleagues examined the nature of restructuring in areas such as classroom instruction and curriculum, professional work life, school governance, and community relations. They also observed the effects of those changes on students' performance, giving special attention to the intellectual quality of their work. The project has yielded important findings, which, when combined with the Lee and Smith studies, make a convincing case for ingredients of restructuring that contribute significantly to students' learning.

Effective classroom instruction. One area of concentration of the School Restructuring Study is a critical look at student achievement to determine whether this desirable outcome actually includes helping students "to use their minds well," a central Coalition principle. Newmann and his colleagues had expressed concern that without high standards of intellectual quality, innovative classroom techniques could promote active engagement by students in superficial or meaningless pursuits. They wanted to be certain that they could measure whether student accomplishments in restructuring schools are, as called for by reformers, "significant, worthwhile and meaningful" (Newmann, Marks, and Gamoran, in press, p. 3).

Since success on standardized achievement tests fails to demonstrate the range of valued intellectual skills, Newmann and his colleagues began by developing criteria for intellectual achievement, which they called authentic achievement. They established three criteria for authentic achievement. Construction of knowledge requires producing meaning or knowledge, instead of merely retrieving the meaning or knowledge produced by others. Disciplined inquiry entails using prior knowledge, striving for in-depth understanding rather than superficial awareness, and expressing conclusions through elaborated communication. Value beyond school ensures that the accomplishment has meaning beyond simply proving success in school (Newmann, Secada, and Wehlage, 1995).

The researchers then developed standards for classroom instruction, which they called authentic pedagogy, to match classroom content, methods of instruction, and assessment tasks with the goal of authentic student performance.

Their criteria for authentic achievement and pedagogy echo many of the Coalition's nine common principles, including directing curricular decisions toward students' attempts to gain mastery rather than teachers' efforts to cover content, viewing students as workers, and protecting the school's central intellectual purpose.

Based on these criteria and standards, scoring systems were created to evaluate lessons and assessment tasks as well as student performance. The research team used them to observe and evaluate mathematics and social studies classes, rate assessment tasks, and grade student work.

It is worth quoting the authors themselves about their findings: "We offer new evidence . . . that authentic pedagogy pays off in improved student performance, and can improve student performance regardless of gender, race, ethnicity or socioeconomic status. The results were consistent across different grades and subjects in schools across the United States. Until now, arguments in support of 'authentic' teaching have often been made on philosophical grounds. We believe this study offers some of the strongest empirical justification to date for pursuing such a course" (Newmann, Marks, and Gamoran, 1995, p. 1).

These findings, especially when coupled with the Lee and Smith studies, firmly establish the positive effect of authentic instruction on high-quality student performance and strongly support Coalition beliefs. But a closer look can also serve as a reminder of how difficult it is to implement the necessary changes. Even in the most successful classrooms, the instruction was rated well below the highest possible rating for authentic pedagogy (7.5 out of a possible 12). This discovery calls for vigilance in identifying and supporting practices inside and outside the classroom that promote standards of intellectual rigor.

Professional community. Having established the link between authentic instruction and the increased intellectual capacity of students, the School Restructuring Study researchers asked the same question as Lee, Smith, and Croninger: what organizational characteristics promote this type of instruction? The researchers found that the most important factor in organizational capacity is the presence of a strong professional community. Further, they found that on their measures of authentic student achievement, student learning was significantly affected by the level of professional community. In a professional community, teachers pursue a clear shared purpose for all students' learning, engage in collaborative work to achieve that purpose, and take collective responsibility for student learning. In their summary of the study, Newmann and Wehlage interpret the impact of professional community as follows: "Overall, if we compared two 'average' students, one in a school with low teacher professional community, and the other in a school with high professional community, the students in a high community school would score about 27 percent higher on the School Restructuring Study measure" (Newmann and Wehlage, 1995, p. 30).

The indicators used in the School Restructuring Study to determine the level of professional community closely matched three of the organizational features identified by Lee, Smith, and Croninger — pursuit of a common curriculum, collective responsibility, and academic press — thereby adding to the strength of their findings.

Summing It Up

In the summary report of the Center on Organization and Restructuring of Schools' five-year study, Newmann and Wehlage offer a succinct characterization of the relationship among the variables they studied in restructuring schools. They call it the "circles of support." High-quality student learning resides in the center — the core activity of the school.

Authentic instruction, the next circle of support, directly influences high-quality learning. It in turn is affected by the school's organizational capacity — particularly the level of professional community. The school's organizational capacity is influenced by the outer circle, the degree of external support from parents, the community, and the district, state, and federal levels (1995, p. 2).

This view of the context for effective school restructuring is instructive for Coalition schools. Through their nine common principles, the schools strive to realize Newmann and Wehlage's vision of high-quality student learning and authentic instruction. The communal orientation of Coalition schools promotes conditions for professional community. The reported importance of the outer circle — external supports — is a helpful reminder of the practical conditions that can promote or undermine a school's efforts.

Assessing a Belief-Driven Reform Effort

A second long-term project, under the direction of Robert Felner, is being conducted by the University of Illinois Center for Prevention Research and Development for the Carnegie Foundation. Over a six- to seven-year period, Felner and his associates are following more than fifty middle schools in Illinois as they move toward implementing recommendations of the Carnegie Council's Task Force on the Education of Young Adolescents, presented in the 1989 report *Turning Points*. Four of the eight recommendations match Coalition principles. They call upon schools to create small communities of learning, teach a core academic program, ensure success for all students, and empower teachers and administrators within the school to make decisions.

Because of the strikingly similar goals of *Turning Points* and the Coalition of Essential Schools, this assessment of another belief-driven reform effort is of particular value. The study has other promising features as well. Its six- to seven-year time frame, the longest of any study to date, will yield new information about restructuring efforts. In addition, the researchers will be identifying the effects of specific restructuring practices and analyzing which components and combination of components lead to greater outcomes.

As schools move toward implementing the *Turning Points* recommendations, the study will track changes in student academic achievement, socioemotional and behavioral adjustment, and school experiences. It will also report how variations and forms of implementation affect outcomes for students at risk and the degree to which the impact varies in different school contexts.

Using a compressed longitudinal design, Felner and his associates will track schools at different levels of experience with *Turning Points* reforms. By admitting a group of new schools into the sample each year, the researchers can observe whether the newer groups show similar patterns of changes to those that precede them. In 1991 the study began with 11 schools, 357 staff, 4548 students, and 11 administrators. As of 1994 the sample had been increased to 52 schools, 1446 staff, 25,434 students, and 72 administrators.

The schools have been classified into three levels of implementation. High-level schools have accomplished a majority of the structural changes in ways that reflect the beliefs of *Turning Points*. Partial-level schools have implemented at least some key structural changes at high levels but not as many or as systematically. No-implementation schools have as yet made no changes.

Felner and his associates have published their findings from the first three years (in press). Confirming the results of earlier studies, they found that across subject areas on the Illinois state achievement tests, students in highly implemented schools achieved at much higher levels than those in nonimplemented schools and substantially better than those in partially implemented schools. Upon closer examination, the news is even better. The scores as reported combine sixth and eighth grades. When the eighth-grade scores are viewed alone, the differences are stronger, suggesting that the longer students are exposed to the conditions, the greater the impact those conditions have. This pattern of differences between levels of implementation appeared also in teacher reports of student behavior problems and student self-reports. In addition, longitudinal data show that whatever the preexisting levels of student outcomes in these areas, as schools move through levels of implementation of the *Turning Points* recommendations, there are associated gains in key areas of student functioning.

As mentioned earlier, Felner and his associates have determined that the sequence and degree of structural changes such as teaming and advisory periods — which are common in Coalition schools — significantly affect the desired outcomes. They have been able to identify patterns of elements within those structures that appear to have a significant association with which goals can be accomplished. For example, they report that for genuine instructional changes to take place, teaming must include a common planning period in addition to individual planning time on a daily basis. Reduced levels, especially below three days per week, result in a far slower level of instructional change. Further, it appears that there are critical levels below or above which no difference or even a negative effect is found. They report that "teams that exceed approximately 120 students, that have fewer than four common planning periods per week, and that have student/teacher ratios beyond the middle twenties tend to show little impact on instructional practices or student well-being . . . And without common planning time, even with small teams of students, actual instruction does not appear to change" (Felner et al., in press, p. 30).

Since many Coalition schools implement teaming, advisory periods, and other practices being observed in the study, its continuing yield will be extremely valuable.

Viewing Individual Schools

Another set of studies that provides helpful information about student performance in restructuring Coalition or like-minded schools has been undertaken by the National Center for Restructuring Education, Schools, and Teaching (NCREST) at Teachers College, Columbia University. The center, founded in 1990 and codirected by Ann Lieberman and Linda Darling-Hammond, supports the creation and studies the progress of "schools that are learner-centered, enriched by teachers' learning opportunities and supported by assessment practices that inspire continuous improvement" (Lieberman, 1995, p. 1). Although they focus on case studies of individual schools rather than on achievement data across schools, NCREST researchers have studied more than fifteen schools, a large percentage of which are Coalition schools. Their continued focus on performance assessment and Exhibitions has offered unique insights into the application of this Coalition principle.

In a compilation of studies documenting the uses of performance assessments in six Coalition schools, Darling-Hammond, Ancess, and Falk (1995) identified several common themes. The implementation of authentic assessment as an integral part of the school program had a positive impact on teacher practice, student performance, and school organization. Teachers in all schools reported that their experiences looking at students' work "deliberatively and collectively" (p. 253) deepened their understanding of the nature of student learning and created the need to change their teaching practices. Student and teacher testimony from all of the schools points to the fact that as students who usually did poorly gained access to knowledge and opportunities to learn, "their productivity and motivation have increased and the quality of their work has risen" (p. 260). And in all the schools, the new assessment practices created a need to reorganize traditional school structures such as class schedules and faculty roles.

The problems and triumphs of the schools described in all of these case studies provide a convincing picture of the power of the Coalition principle that calls for students to demonstrate or exhibit the quality and breadth of their intellectual performance prior to graduation.

Some Implications

All of the studies confirm both the promise of the Coalition's work and its complexity. In Kyle's evaluation of the Jefferson County schools, Newmann and his colleagues' examination of authentic pedagogy, and Felner and his associates' assessment of the restructuring in *Turning Points* schools, the higher the level of implementation, the more positive the effects on student achievement. Yet in the latter two studies it was clear that even the schools exhibiting the highest levels of implementation had a lot further to go before implementation could be considered total.

The perils involved in implementation are apparent in another large-scale study, conducted by Sam Stringfield and his colleagues at Johns Hopkins Center for the Social Organization of Schools. This study, entitled Special Strategies for Educating Disadvantaged Children, explores ten promising programs over a three-year period for the U.S. Department of Education Chapter One program. Included are the Coalition of Essential Schools, Comer's School Development Program, and Slavin's Success for All, among others. While the final report, which will include data on student outcomes, is not yet available, the interim report echoes others' concerns about the difficulties of implementation. One of the fourteen first-year observations asserts "an easy mistake would be to believe that any of the schools in the Special Strategies studies is now 'doing [its strategy] right' . . . These implementations are proving to be highly dynamic and that finding underscores the wisdom of building [these studies] as longitudinal studies" (Stringfield and Winfield, 1994, p. vi).

In their report, Felner and his associates make some further observations about the process of implementation. Often the first year of implementation includes a fair degree of disruption, and it may take another one or two years for the changes to become institutionalized. Five or more years' experience of institutionalized changes may be required before a cohort of students shows maximum differences in behavior. They also note that for "at risk" students, the majority of gains are not realized until the implementation is quite mature. These observations strengthen the position of many educators who urge sticking with changes that might not yet be showing desired results.

It is reassuring to know that the direction of the restructuring efforts is decidedly positive. But it is also a strong reminder to the Coalition of the degree to which the schools require continued assistance and persistence. In summary, Sizer's Horace Smith can feel confident that his school is headed in a direction that will significantly benefit students. But the path can be twisting and difficult. He and his colleagues will need to have a clear sense of their goal and to make a persistent effort to find their way.

References

Bryk, A. S., and Driscoll, M. E. 1988. *High school as community: Contextual influences, and consequences for students and teachers.* Madison, Wis.: National Center for Effective Secondary Schools.

Carnegie Council for Adolescent Development. 1989. *Turning Points.* Washington, D.C.: Carnegie Council for Adolescent Development.

Cushman, K. 1995. What research suggests about Essential school ideas. *Horace* (11) 3: 1–5, 7.

Darling-Hammond, L., Ancess, J., and Falk, B. 1995. *Authentic assessment in action: Studies of schools and students at work.* New York: Teachers College Press.

Felner, R. D., Jackson, A., Kasak, D., Mulhall, P., Brand, S., and Flowers, N. In press. The impact of school reform for the middle years: A longitudinal study of a network engaged in *Turning Points*–based comprehensive school transformation. In R. Takanishi and D. Hamburg (eds.), *Preparing young adolescents for the 21st century: Challenges for Europe and the United States.* New York: Cambridge University Press.

Kyle, R. 1993. Transforming our schools: Lessons from the Jefferson County Public Schools/Gheens Professional Development Academy 1983–1991. Louisville, Ky.: Gheens Foundation.

Lee, V. E., Bryk, A. S., and Smith, J. B. 1993. The organization of effective secondary schools. In L. Darling-Hammond (ed.), *Review of Research in Education* 19: 171–267. Washington, D.C.: American Educational Research Association.

Lee, V. E., and Smith, J. B. 1994a. High school restructuring and student achievement: A new study finds strong links. *Issues in Restructuring Schools* 7: 1–5, 16. Madison, Wis.: Center on Organization and Restructuring of Schools.

———. 1994b. *Effects of high school restructuring and size on gains in achievement and engagement for early secondary school students.* Madison, Wis.: Center on Organization and Restructuring of Schools.

Lee, V. E., Smith, J. B., and Croninger, R. G. 1995a. Another look at high school restructuring. *Issues in Restructuring Schools* 9: 5–10. Madison, Wis.: Center on Organization and Restructuring of Schools.

————. 1995b. *Understanding high school restructuring effects on the equitable distribution of learning in mathematics and science.* Madison, Wis.: Center on Organization and Restructuring of Schools.

Lieberman, A. (ed.). 1995. *The work of restructuring schools: Building from the ground up.* New York: Teachers College Press.

Newmann, F. M., Marks, H. M., and Gamoran, A. In press. Authentic pedagogy and student performance. *American Journal of Education.*

————. 1995. Authentic pedagogy: Standards that boost student performance. *Issues in Restructuring Schools* 8: 1–12. Madison, Wis.: Center on Organization and Restructuring of Schools.

Newmann, F. M., Secada, W. G., and Wehlage, G. G. 1995. *A guide to authentic instruction and assessment: Vision, standards, and scoring.* Madison, Wis.: Center on Organization and Restructuring of Schools.

Newmann, F. M., and Wehlage, G. G. 1995. *Successful school restructuring: A report to the public and educators by the Center on Organization and Restructuring of Schools.* Madison, Wis.: Center on Organization and Restructuring of Schools.

Stringfield, S., and Winfield, L. 1994. *Urban and suburban/rural special strategies for educating disadvantaged children: First year report.* Washington, D.C.: U. S. Department of Education.

Appendix C

Members of the Coalition of Essential Schools

As of March 1996, the following schools were partners in the Coalition of Essential Schools. These schools have completed the Coalition's membership process and are implementing new practices based on the nine common principles of Essential schools. There are also 790 schools affiliated with the Coalition as either planning or exploring schools.

Alaska
Paul T. Albert Memorial School
Tununak

Arkansas
Ridgecrest High School
Paragould

Perryville High School
Perryville

Sheridan Junior High School
Sheridan

Siloam Springs High School
Siloam Springs

Springdale High School
Springdale

California
Homestead High School
Cupertino

Irvington High School
Fremont

Rancho San Joaquin Middle School
Irvine

South Lake Middle School
Irvine

Alexander Hamilton Middle School
Long Beach

Hollenbeck Middle School
Los Angeles

Oceana High School
Pacifica

Mid-Peninsula High School
Palo Alto

Pasadena High School
Pasadena

Spring View Middle School
Rocklin

Herbert Hoover High School
San Diego

O'Farrell Community School
San Diego

James Lick Middle School
San Francisco

Lincoln Middle School
Santa Monica

Piner High School
Santa Rosa

Torrance High School
Torrance

Whittier High School
Whittier

Colorado
Pueblo County High School
Pueblo

Skyview High School
Thornton

Connecticut
Watkinson School
Hartford

Weaver High School
Hartford

Rippowam Magnet Middle School
Stamford

Delaware
Middletown High School
Middletown

Brookside Elementary School
Newark

Hodgson Vo-Tech High School
Newark

Seaford Middle School
Seaford

Phoenix Academy at Wilmington
   High School
Wilmington

Florida
Coral Springs Elementary School
Coral Springs

Coral Springs Middle School
Coral Springs

Westchester Elementary School
Coral Springs

Nova Blanche Forman
Elementary School
Davie

Nova D. D. Eisenhower
Elementary School
Davie

Nova High School
Davie

Nova Middle School
Davie

Silver Ridge Elementary School
Davie

Meadowbrook Elementary
School
Fort Lauderdale

University School of Nova
Southeastern U.
Fort Lauderdale

Sheridan Academy of Applied
Technology
Hollywood

Centennial Middle School
Miami

Coral Reef Elementary School
Miami

Cutler Ridge Middle School
Miami

William Lehman Elementary
School
Miami

William Turner Technical Arts
High School
Miami

John F. Kennedy Middle School
North Miami Beach

Oakland Park Elementary School
Oakland Park

Norcrest Elementary School
Pompano Beach

Pompano Beach Elementary School
Pompano Beach

Pompano Beach Middle School
Pompano Beach

Georgia
Ben Franklin Academy
Atlanta

Memorial Middle School
Conyers

Salem High School
Conyers

Counterpane School
Fayetteville

Hawaii
Maryknoll High School
Honolulu

Iowa
Metro High School
Cedar Rapids

Illinois
Anna-Jonesboro High School
Anna

Carpentersville Middle School
Carpentersville

Calumet High School
Chicago

Chicago Vocational High School
Chicago

DuSable High School
Chicago

Englewood High School
Chicago

Flower Vocational High School
Chicago

Lindblom Technical High School
Chicago

Mather High School
Chicago

Paul Robeson High School
Chicago

Steinmetz Academic Centre
Chicago

Sullivan High School
Chicago

Wendell Phillips High School
Chicago

Elmwood Junior/Senior
    High School
Elmwood

North Middle School
Godfrey

Malta Junior/Senior High School
Malta

Broadmoor Junior High School
Pekin

Roosevelt Middle School
River Forest

Lake Park High School
Roselle

Sparta High School
Sparta

Indiana
Madison Heights High School
Anderson

Harmony School
Bloomington

South Vermillion Middle School
Clinton

Hibberd Middle School
Richmond

Chauncey Rose Middle School
Terre Haute

Kentucky
Ballard High School
Louisville

Conway Middle School
Louisville

Doss High School
Louisville

Eastern High School
Louisville

Fairdale High School
Louisville

Iroquois High School
Louisville

J. Graham Brown School
Louisville

Seneca High School
Louisville

Valley High School
Louisville

Western High School
Louisville

Pleasure Ridge Park High School
Pleasure Ridge Park

Mayme S. Waggener High School
St. Matthews

Maine
Noble High School
Berwick

Gorham High School
Gorham

Maryland
Bryn Mawr School
Baltimore

Walbrook High School
Baltimore

Massachusetts
Fenway Middle College
    High School
Boston

Brimmer and May School
Chestnut Hill

Ralph B. O'Maley Middle School
Gloucester

Bartlett Middle School
Lowell

Northampton High School
Northampton

Collins Middle School
Salem

Mount Everett Regional School
Sheffield

Ware High School
Ware

Michigan
Caledonia High School
Caledonia

Northport Public School
Northport

Missouri

Belton High School
Belton

McCluer High School
Florissant

Kirkwood High School
Kirkwood

Parkway South High School
Manchester

North Kansas City High School
North Kansas City

Ritenour Senior High School
Overland

A. B. Green Middle School
Richmond Heights

Greenwood Lab School
Springfield

Parkview High School
Springfield

Hoech Middle School
St. Ann

Whitfield School
St. Louis

University City High School
University City

Windsor Junior/Senior High School
Windsor

New Hampshire

Souhegan High School
Amherst

Thayer High School
Winchester

New Jersey

Academy for the Advancement of
    Science and Technology
Hackensack

Bergen County Technical
    High School
Hackensack

New Mexico

Cleveland Middle School
Albuquerque

West Mesa High School
Albuquerque

Bernalillo High School
Bernalillo

Bernalillo Middle School
Bernalillo

Capital High School
Santa Fe

Capshaw Middle School
Santa Fe

Sweeney Elementary School
Santa Fe

La Plata Middle School
Silver City

Roosevelt Middle School
Tijeras

Twin Buttes High School
Zuni

New York
Fox Lane High School
Bedford

Bronx New School
Bronx

Schomburg Satellite Academy
    Bronx
Bronx

University Heights High School
Bronx

Bronxville High School
Bronxville

Metropolitan Corporate Academy
Brooklyn

The Brooklyn New School
Brooklyn

The New Program at P.S. 261
Brooklyn

Chatham High School
Chatham

Croton-Harmon High School
Croton-on-Hudson

Pierre Van Cortlandt Middle
    School
Croton-on-Hudson

The Village School
Great Neck

Alternative Community School
Ithaca

Belle Sherman Elementary School
Ithaca

International High School
Long Island City

Middle College High School
Long Island City

Central Park East I
New York

Central Park East II
New York

Central Park East Secondary
    School
New York

Coalition School for Social Change
New York

Community Service Academy
New York

Crossroads School
New York

Earth School — P.S. 364
New York

Institute for Collaborative
  Education
New York

Landmark High School
New York

Lower East Side School
New York

Manhattan International
  High School
New York

Manhattan Village Academy
  High School
New York

Muscota New School
New York

Neighborhood School
New York

P.S. 234, Independence School
New York

Public School Repertory Company
New York

River East Elementary School
New York

Satellite Academy — Chambers
  Site
New York

Satellite Academy — Forsythe Site
New York

School for Academic and Athletic
  Excellence
New York

School of the Future
New York

The Center School
New York

The Computer School
New York

The Early Childhood Center
New York

Urban Academy
New York

Vanguard High School
New York

School Without Walls
Rochester

Scarsdale Alternative School
Scarsdale

Southampton High School
Southampton

Ohio

Woodward High School
Cincinnati

Independence High School
Columbus

Gilmour Academy
Gates Mills

Reynoldsburg High School
Reynoldsburg

Federal Hocking High School
Stewart

Oklahoma
Westminster Middle School
Oklahoma City

Pennsylvania
Bellefonte Area Senior High School
Bellefonte

Central Bucks High School East
Buckingham

A. K. McClure Elementary School
Philadelphia

Alternative for the Middle Years
　　(AMY 6)
Philadelphia

Bayard Taylor Elementary School
Philadelphia

The Crefeld School
Philadelphia

Rhode Island
Central Falls Junior/Senior
　　High School
Central Falls

St. Xavier Academy
Coventry

The Gordon School
East Providence

Narragansett Elementary School
Narragansett

Narragansett Pier School
Narragansett

Narragansett Senior High School
Narragansett

Hope High School
Providence

Rhode Island School for the Deaf
Providence

School One
Providence

Kickemuit Middle School
Warren

South Carolina
Heathwood Hall Episcopal School
Columbia

Dutch Fork High School
Irmo

Socastee High School
Myrtle Beach

Central High School
Pageland

Tennessee
Hixson High School
Chattanooga

St. Andrew's–Sewanee School
St. Andrews

Texas
Paschal High School
Fort Worth

Westbury High School
Houston

The Judson Montessori School
San Antonio

Vermont
Gailer School
Middlebury

Virginia
York High School
Yorktown

Washington
Newport Heights Elementary
    School
Bellevue

Henry M. Jackson High School
Bothell

Gig Harbor High School
Gig Harbor

Finn Hill Junior High School
Kirkland

Puyallup High School
Puyallup

Eastlake High School
Redmond

Inglewood Junior High School
Redmond

Jemtegaard Middle School
Washougal

Wisconsin
Burlington High School
Burlington

Riverside University High School
Milwaukee

Walden III
Racine

Canada
Bishop Carroll High School
Calgary, Alberta

England
Hugh Christie Technology College
Tonbridge, Kent

Uckfield Community College
Uckfield, East Sussex

Acknowledgments

With a book of this kind, a writer's debt to friends is both wide and deep. *Horace's Hope* is not the result of a controlled research design. Rather, it is the best that I could create from exposure to a tapestry of impressions — voices, images, and opinions drawn from many quarters as I plied a number of full-time and related jobs: administering the Coalition of Essential Schools, attending to the birth of the Annenberg Institute for School Reform, helping with Walter Annenberg's remarkable Challenge to the Nation for serious reform of the public schools, teaching undergraduate students at Brown, and, above all, traveling among the schools to help, listen, watch, and try to make sense.

Given this reach for sources, a simple, definitive list of attribution and thanks is not wholly possible. Thanks in general are possible, surely, and they go to countless people who had the grace and generosity to let me into their work, to talk with me, to suggest matters to read and ponder, to argue with me. Schools, happily, are full of such people.

On the text itself, I had a great deal of help. Several good friends read multiple drafts and gave me telling criticism, especially Nancy Sizer, Ansley Erickson, Arthur Powell, Barbara Powell, Mike Rose, Deborah Meier, Dennis Littky, Jim Cullen (who suggested the title for Chapter 1), Lyde Cullen Sizer, Alice Sizer Warner, Amy Kantrowitz, Joe McDonald, Patricia Wasley, Rick Lear, Paula Evans, Ken White, and my editors at Houghton Mifflin, Wendy Strothman, Wendy Holt, Liz Duvall, Gail Winston, and Hilary Liftin. That all of these, and others, did not agree on the specifics was particularly helpful: the conflicting counsel highlighted where some of the conundrums lay. That the resulting volume does not reflect every bit of advice from each goes without saying. The final judgments and arguments are my sole responsibility.

Kathy Hardie, Pat Strickland, Amy Kantrowitz, and Ansley Erickson generously carried myriad loads for Horace at the offices at Brown. Ansley took special responsibility for assembling the final notes and for getting the evidence right. My joy is being part of a team (dubbed "the chairman's office") which is never afraid of hard work, never visibly exasperated with the dottiness of the chairman, and always keeps its sense of humor.

Peggy MacMullen consented to write the appendix on the research record about Essential schools. An independent and skilled researcher on these matters was necessary, and I am grateful to her for taking on this detailed and important work.

Formal and informal seminars served me well. The seminar associated with the ATLAS project (supported by the New American Schools Development Corporation), which joined the Coalition with colleagues at Yale, Harvard, Education Development Center, and the public schools of Prince George's County, Maryland, Norfolk, Virginia, and Gorham, Maine, was especially useful. The formal ATLAS seminar gave focus to particular chapters in *Horace's Hope;* I am very much in the debt here of Howard Gardner, Janet Whitla, James Comer, Bethany Rogers, Tom Hatch, and Veronica Boix-Mansilla.

Seemingly weekly talks with Deborah Meier, usually via the miracles of telephone or fax, have kept my priorities straight. Regular conversation with Frank Newman from the Education Commission of the States, usually by phone when Frank was fogbound in some remote airport, were always stimulating. Equally and happily endless work took place with key Coalition colleagues at Brown — Ed Campbell, Paula Evans, Bob McCarthy, Joe McDonald, Barbara Cervone, and Don Ernst, among a goodly horde of others. Students in my classes were more helpful in sharpening my ideas than they might have been aware, especially those in our traveling seminar, which spent each spring shadowing elementary and secondary school students from Delaware to Maine in a wide variety of schools.

However, no "seminar" was more important than that encompassed by my marriage of forty-one years to Nancy Sizer. She is a teacher's teacher, soaked in the realities of schools and in their potentials and joys. She knows adolescents, and we talk of them and their schools endlessly. I trust that I have learned well and will continue to learn from her.

I depend on a happy base at Brown University, and the support I have received here from President Vartan Gregorian and Provost Frank Rothman has been sustained, informed, generous, and thus crucially important. My colleagues in the education department, and especially our chairman, Tom James, have been good and patient friends.

For over a decade, more than a score of private foundations and public agencies have supported the work of the Coalition of Essential Schools, by direct grants either to the schools or to our unit at Brown University. Without this help, none of the work of which I write would have been possible. In addition to several important anonymous donors, let me record alphabetically those organizations that have taken a risk to support us all over the past eleven years: Aaron Diamond Foundation; Aetna Institute for Corporate Education; the Ahmanson Foundation; George I. Alden Trust; the Annenberg Foundation; ARCO Foundation; the Arthur Vinings Davis Foundation; AT&T Foundation; Carnegie Corporation of New York; Circuit City Foundation; Citibank, N.A; Charles E. Culpepper Foundation, Inc.; the Danforth Foundation; DeWitt Wallace–Reader's Digest Fund; Joseph Drown Foundation; Emerson Electric Company; Exxon Education Foundation; Geraldine R. Dodge Foundation; the Hearst Foundation; William Randolph Hearst Foundation; William and Flora Hewlett Foundation; the Richard L. Hirsch Foundation, Inc.; IBM Corporation; the Johnson Foundation; W. Alton Jones Foundation; Joyce Foundation; E. A. & J. Klingenstein Fund, Inc.; Kraft General Foods; the Henry Luce Foundation; John D. and Catherine T. MacArthur Foundation; the Andrew W. Mellon Foundation; Melville Corporation; Merillat Foundation; Monsanto Fund; State of Missouri; National Center for Restructuring Education, Schools, and Teaching; National Center for Science Teaching and Learning; National

Science Foundation; New American Schools Development Corporation; Edward John Noble Foundation; Noyce Foundation; Pacific Telesis Foundation; the David and Lucile Packard Foundation; the Pew Charitable Trusts; RJR Nabisco Foundation; Rockefeller Brothers Fund; the Rockefeller Foundation; the San Francisco Foundation; SBC Foundation; Spencer Foundation; the United Parcel Services Foundation; Xerox Foundation.

Notes

Preface: Horace Smith

1. Jonathan Kozol, *Savage Inequalities: Children in America's Schools* (New York: Trumpet, 1992).

1. A Story Where Nothing Happens

1. My field notes are largely as I first prepared them. Only some noncrucial elements have been changed to mask identities.
2. See Diane Ravitch, *National Standards in American Education: A Citizen's Guide* (Washington, D.C.: Brookings Institution, 1995), pp. 94–97, and U.S. Department of Education, National Center for Education Statistics, "High School Course Taking in the Core Subject Areas," *Indicator of the Month,* June 1994.
3. See Arthur G. Powell, Eleanor Farrar, and David K. Cohen, *The Shopping Mall High School: Winners and Losers in the Educational Marketplace* (Boston: Houghton Mifflin, 1985), Ch. 2.
4. U.S. Department of Education, National Center for Education Statistics, *The Condition of Education 1994* (Washington, D.C.: U.S. Government Printing Office, 1994), p. 132.
5. In 1970, 76.9 percent of seventeen-year-olds were high school graduates, compared to 73.1 percent in 1994. U.S. Department of Education, National

Center for Education Statistics, *Digest of Education Statistics 1994* (Washington, D.C.: U.S. Government Printing Office, 1994), p. 108.

6. NAEP reading performance of seventeen-year-olds increased four points (on a scale of 0–500) from 1980 to 1992, math performance increased eight points from 1982 to 1992, and science performance increased eleven points from 1982 to 1992, while eleventh-graders' performance in writing declined two points from 1984 to 1992. U.S. Department of Education, *Digest of Education Statistics 1994,* pp. 113–27.

7. Average verbal SAT score for college-bound seniors was 424 in both 1980 and 1993, with a variation of no more than seven points during those years. Math scores ranged from 466 in 1980 to 478 in 1993. All scores are recorded on a 0–800 scale. U.S. Department of Education, *Digest of Education Statistics 1994,* p. 128.

8. While 133,702 high school students (less than one percent of the total high school student population) took 178,519 AP examinations in 1980, 447,972 students (3.2 percent of the total population) took 684,449 examinations in 1994. Advanced Placement Program, College Board, *National Summary Reports 1994,* p. 3; Advanced Placement Program, *Advanced Placement Program Statistical Tables, 1991–92,* p. 1; and National Center for Education Statistics, *Digest of Education Statistics 1994,* p. 11.

9. While average per-pupil expenditure has risen from $3895 in 1980 to an estimated $5327 in 1993 (in constant 1993–1994 dollars) — an increase of 36 percent — much of this increase can be attributed to dramatic increases in teacher salaries and expenditures on special education. Teacher salaries increased 21.7 percent from 1980 to 1993, and special education students increased in number from 8.5 percent of the total public school enrollment in 1980 to 11.7 percent in 1993. National Center for Education Statistics, *Digest of Education Statistics 1994,* p. 151; U.S. Department of Education, National Center for Education Statistics, "Salaries of Teachers," *Indicator of the Month,* May 1995; and U.S. Department of Education, National Center for Education Statistics, "Education of Students with Disabilities," *Indicator of the Month,* February 1995. An investigation into spending trends, which concludes that the expenditure for "regular" students remains virtually flat, is Richard Rothstein and Karen Hawley Miles, *Where's the Money Gone? Changes in the Level and Composition of Education Spending* (Washington, D.C.: Economic Policy Institute, 1995).

2. There Is More to It than Just the Schools

1. Milbrey McLaughlin and Merita A. Irby, "Urban Sanctuaries: Neighborhood Organizations That Keep Hope Alive," *Phi Delta Kappan* (December 1994): 300–6.
2. U.S. Bureau of the Census, *Statistical Abstract of the United States 1994* (Washington, D.C.: U.S. Government Printing Office, 1994), p. 475.
3. Janice Hamilton Outz, *The Demographics of American Families* (Washington, D.C.: Institute for Educational Leadership, 1993), p. 8.
4. Alan Gutmacher Institute, *Sex and America's Teenagers* (New York: Alan Gutmacher Institute, 1994), pp. 45, 55.
5. Between nine and twelve million adolescents have no health coverage, and millions of others have inadequate coverage. Only approximately 55 percent would seek health care if pregnant, even without parental knowledge. Fred Hechinger, *Fateful Choices: Healthy Youth for the 21st Century* (New York: Hill and Wang, 1992), pp. 37–42. See Ch. 4 for data on alcohol, tobacco, and other drug use.
6. U.S. Bureau of the Census, *Statistical Abstract 1994,* Table 126.
7. Carnegie Council on Adolescent Development, Task Force on Education of Young Adolescents, *Turning Points: Preparing American Youth for the 21st Century: Recommendations for Transforming Middle Grade Schools* (Washington, D.C.: Carnegie Council on Adolescent Development, 1990).

3. The Words of Reform

1. Herbert Kohl, *"I Won't Learn from You" and Other Thoughts on Creative Maladjustment* (New York: New Press, 1994).
2. The fullest and most persuasive outline of systemic reform is Marshall S. Smith and Jennifer A. O'Day, "Systemic School Reform," in S. Fuhrman and B. Malen, eds., *The Politics of Curriculum and Testing* (Bristol, Pa.: Falmer, 1991).
3. On this theme see John E. Chubb and Terry M. Moe, *Politics, Markets, and America's Schools* (Washington, D.C.: Brookings Institution, 1990).
4. Gary Orfield, *The Growth of Segregation in American Schools: Changing Patterns of Separation and Poverty since 1968* (Cambridge, Mass.: Harvard University Press, 1994).

5. See David Tyack, *The One Best System: A History of American Urban Education* (Cambridge, Mass.: Harvard University Press, 1974).

6. National Commission on Excellence in Education, *A Nation at Risk* (Washington, D.C.: U.S. Government Printing Office, 1983).

7. Ravitch, *National Standards in American Education,* and Robert Rothman, *Measuring Up: Standards, Assessment and School Reform* (San Francisco: Jossey-Bass, 1995). For a more critical view, see also F. Allan Hanson, *Testing Testing: Social Consequences of the Examined Life* (Berkeley: University of California Press, 1994).

8. My colleagues and I have spelled out one practical answer to the standards issue. See *Horace's School* (Boston: Houghton Mifflin, 1992), Ch. 8, 10, and 11. See also Theodore R. Sizer, Joseph P. McDonald, and Bethany Rogers, "Standards and School Reform: Asking the Basic Questions," *Stanford Law and Policy Review* (Winter 1992–1993): 27–35.

9. See L. Scott Miller, *An American Imperative: Accelerating Minority Educational Achievement* (New Haven, Conn.: Yale University Press, 1995).

10. The reference to the "unspecial majority" is from Powell, Farrar, and Cohen, *The Shopping Mall High School.*

4. The Work of Reform

1. See Michael Lipsky, *Street-Level Bureaucracy: Dilemmas of the Individual in Public Services* (New York: Russell Sage, 1980).

2. On Central Park East Secondary School, see Deborah W. Meier, *The Power of Their Ideas: Lessons for America from a Small School in Harlem* (Boston: Beacon, 1995).

3. See David Tyack and Larry Cuban, *Tinkering Towards Utopia* (Cambridge, Mass.: Harvard University Press, 1995), Ch. 5 and Epilogue.

4. Donna E. Muncey and Patrick J. McQuillan, *Reform and Resistance in Schools and Classrooms* (New Haven, Conn.: Yale University Press, 1996). See also Diana Tittle, *Welcome to Heights High: The Crippling Politics of Restructuring America's Public Schools* (Columbus: Ohio State University Press, 1995).

5. Oregon Department of Education, "Setting Standards for the Certificate of Initial Mastery," Draft 11/1/94, p. 4.

6. These numbers are drawn from conversations with teachers and those who study teaching in these areas.

7. See Paul Hill, "Reinventing Urban Public Education," *Phi Delta Kappan* (January 1994): 396–40, and the New York Networks for School Renewal, Douglas White, director.

8. This reference is from Chester Finn, *We Must Take Charge* (New York: Free Press, 1991), p. 189.

9. Materials about CPESS include Seymour Fliegel and James MacGuire, *Miracle in East Harlem: The Fight for Choice in Public Education* (New York: Free Press, 1993); Meier, *The Power of Their Ideas;* two reports issued by NCREST at Teachers College, Columbia: "Learning to Think Well: Central Park East Secondary School Graduates Reflect on Their High School and College Experiences," by David Bensman, and "Graduation by Portfolio at Central Park East Secondary School," by Linda Darling-Hammond and Jacqueline Ancess; *High School II,* a film of CPESS by Fred Wiseman; *Graduation by Portfolio,* a film produced by CCE; a segment in *Rethinking America,* a PBS video series, and in Hedrick Smith, *Rethinking America* (New York: Random House, 1995).

5. What Matters

1. I have developed these ideas more fully in *Horace's School* (Boston: Houghton Mifflin, 1992), Chs. 6 and 9.

2. See the analysis of recent research related to Coalition ideas by Margaret N. MacMullen, which appears as Appendix B in this volume.

3. See Grant Wiggins, *Assessing Student Performance: Exploring the Purpose and Limits of Testing* (San Francisco: Jossey-Bass, 1993).

4. See David Perkins, *Smart Schools: Better Thinking and Learning for Every Child* (New York: Free Press, 1992).

5. Linda Darling-Hammond, Jacqueline Ancess, and Beverly Falk, *Authentic Assessment in Action* (New York: Teachers College Press, 1995).

6. The Oregon Education Act for the 21st Century, as amended 1995 (Oregon HB 2991).

7. For a telling portrait of this phenomenon and more, see *The Challenge of School Change: Inside One Essential School,* a film and report published by the Merrow Report, South Carolina ETV, and the Coalition of Essential Schools, 1994.

8. See the work of Robert E. Slavin, including *Cooperative Learning* (New York: Longman, 1983) and *Student Team Learning: A Practical Guide to*

Cooperative Learning, 3d ed. (Washington, D.C.: National Education Association, 1991).

9. Howard Gardner and David Perkins of Harvard University and the ATLAS Seminar have helped me a great deal with this argument.

10. Muncey and McQuillan, *Reform and Resistance in Schools and Classrooms.*

11. See Chapter 6, "Small Schools," in Meier, *The Power of Their Ideas,* pp. 107–20. The idea of smallness is spreading, as seen in Chicago's recent incentive to strengthen existing and create new small schools. Ann Bradley, "Chicago Board to Request Proposals for Small Schools," *Education Week,* September 27, 1995, p. 10.

12. See Kathleen Cushman, ed., "A Hard-Pressed School Expects More, Gets More," *Performance* (January 1995), on Oceana High School in Pacifica, California, and Ann Bradley, "Thinking Small," *Education Week,* March 22, 1995, pp. 37–41, on the six small schools created from New York City's Julia Richman High School. See also the four-part *New York Times* series entitled "Multiple Choice: New York's Alternative Schools," which ran from May 22 to May 25, 1995.

13. The work of the School Development Project at Yale University is germane here. See James Comer, *Maggie's American Dream: The Life and Times of a Black Family* (New York: New American Library, 1988), Part II, and *School Power: Implications of an Intervention Project* (New York: Free Press, 1993), especially the epilogue.

14. Muncey and McQuillan, *Reform and Resistance in Schools and Classrooms.*

15. See Appendix B.

16. See Meier, *The Power of Their Ideas.*

17. See Edward B. Fiske, *Smart Schools, Smart Kids* (New York: Simon and Schuster, 1991), and Patricia Wasley's portraits of five teachers in the midst of change, *Stirring the Chalkdust* (New York: Teachers College Press, 1994).

18. See Lipsky, *Street-Level Bureaucracy.*

19. Patricia Wasley, Richard W. Clark, and Robert L. Hampel, *A Collaborative Inquiry on School Change* (Providence: Coalition of Essential Schools, 1995).

20. See Jeannie Oakes, *Keeping Track: How Schools Structure Inequality* (New Haven, Conn.: Yale University Press, 1985), and Anne Wheelock, *Crossing the Tracks: How Untracking Can Save America's Schools* (New York: New Press, 1992).

21. Chapters 8 and 9 of Arthur Powell's volume on independent schools, forthcoming from Harvard University Press, document this matter persuasively.

22. Massachusetts legislation of 1991 provided for the creation of such "break-the-mold" schools by groups of interested citizens statewide. One example is the Francis W. Parker Charter Essential School in Harvard, which opened its doors to students in September 1995.

23. See Appendix B.

24. See David Cohen, "A Revolution in One Classroom: The Case of Mrs. Oublier," *Education Evaluation and Policy Analysis* 12 (3): 311–30.

25. See Muncey and McQuillan, *Reform and Resistance in Schools and Classrooms,* and Seymour B. Sarason, *The Culture of the School and the Problem of Change* (Boston: Allyn and Bacon, 1971).

26. The ATLAS project, currently housed at the Education Development Center in Newton, Massachusetts, represents collaboration on the idea of pathways among individuals from the Coalition of Essential Schools, EDC, Harvard Project Zero, and the Yale School Development Program.

27. New Mexico is a promising example, although the story there is still unfolding. See Education Commission of the States, *State Education Systems in Transition: A Re:Learning Report* (Denver: Education Commission of the States, forthcoming).

6. Troublesome Complexities

1. I am greatly indebted to my colleagues in the ATLAS Seminar, especially Howard Gardner, Bethany Rogers, Veronica Boix-Mansilla, and Barbara Powell, for pushing my thinking on these matters.

2. Perkins, *Smart Schools,* p. 67.

3. Jerome S. Bruner, *The Process of Education* (Cambridge, Mass.: Harvard University Press, 1963).

4. Perkins, *Smart Schools,* p. 45.

5. *The Concord Review* is a journal devoted to publishing distinguished re-

search essays in history written by secondary school students. Will Fitzhugh is the editor, and its offices are in Concord, Massachusetts.

6. Howard Gardner, David Perkins, and their colleagues at Harvard Project Zero have published widely — and persuasively — on this theme. For example, see Perkins, *Smart Schools,* and Howard Gardner, *Multiple Intelligences: The Theories in Practice* (New York: Basic Books, 1993).

7. Howard Gardner, *Frames of Mind: The Theory of Multiple Intelligences* (New York: Basic Books, 1983), pp. 60–61.

8. These lectures were published as Lawrence A. Cremin, *Public Education* (New York: Basic Books, 1976). See also Laurence Steinberg, *Beyond the Classroom: Why School Reform Has Failed and What Parents Need to Do* (New York: Simon and Schuster, 1996).

9. See Howard D. Mehlinger, *School Reform in the Information Age* (Bloomington, Ind.: Center for Excellence in Education, 1995).

7. *Horace's Hope*

1. See David Bensman, *Lives of the Graduates of Central Park East Elementary School: Where Have They Gone? What Did They Really Learn?* (New York: National Center for Restructuring Teaching and Learning, 1994).

2. William Celis, "Annenberg to Give Education $500 Million over Five Years," *New York Times,* December 17, 1993, p. 16.

3. This idea of systems of schools, or networks, has been most fully developed by colleagues in the New York Networks for School Renewal. I am personally grateful for the ideas of Deborah Meier, Paul T. Hill, and Robert McCarthy. A critical issue for such networks is the basis and mechanism for public accountability. Americans have traditionally depended on test scores and other readily collectible data. Another approach is persuasively described by Thomas A. Wilson in *Reaching for a Better Standard: How English Inspection Provokes the Way Americans Know and Judge Schools* (New York: Teachers College Press, 1996).

4. *William G. Milliken, Governor of Michigan, et al.* v. *Ronald Bradley and Richard Bradley; The Grosse Point Public School System* v. *Ronald Bradley and Richard Bradley.* United States Supreme Court, 418 U.S. 717, decided 1974.